the WILD invitation

A 7-SESSION BIBLE STUDY ON THE BOOK OF ACTS

MAC BRIDGES
AND KENZ DURHAM

BETHANYHOUSE
a division of Baker Publishing Group
Minneapolis, Minnesota

Published by Bethany House Publishers
Minneapolis, Minnesota
BethanyHouse.com

Bethany House Publishers is a division of
Baker Publishing Group, Grand Rapids, Michigan

Printed in the United States of America

ISBN 9780764246289 (paper)
ISBN 9781493453863 (ebook)

Library of Congress Cataloging-in-Publication Control Number: 2025025316

Designed by Mac Bridges

The authors are represented by Alive Literary Agency, AliveLiterary.com.

Baker Publishing Group publications use paper produced from sustainable forestry practices and postconsumer waste whenever possible.

25 26 27 28 29 30 31 7 6 5 4 3 2 1

CONTENTS

WEEK FOUR (ACTS 10–13)

WEEK FIVE (ACTS 13–19)

WEEK SIX (ACTS 20–24)

WEEK SEVEN (ACTS 25–28)

Introduction
and How to Use This Study Through the Book of Acts

Introduction

Hi! We're Mac and Kenz, the voices behind this study. We're best friends, kingdom dreamers, and probably a lot like you. In college, we started a Christ-centered community for women called Delight Ministries that's now on more than two hundred college campuses across the country.

These days we're busy juggling being wives, moms, podcasters, and creators of Bible studies and resources largely for women in college and throughout their twenties. But that doesn't mean women in all seasons of life can't grow through this study—you can!

We're so honored to guide you on this journey through the book of Acts. As we do, we'll also be sharing personal stories and diving into the Scripture *with* you.

Mac

- Hometown: Charlotte, North Carolina
- Lover of chain restaurants
- Most likely to use big words and run-on sentences in this study
- Trying to go pro in pickleball when she's not "momming it" or writing Bible studies

Kenz

- Hometown: Vero Beach, Florida
- The one with the Valley girl accent
- Most likely to make you laugh while you're reading this study
- A crunchy mom (you know, leaning toward all the natural) who also has a hidden candy stash at all times

Here's a sentence you've probably never read at the start of a Bible study: *We're headed straight for danger.* But stick with us. In the upside-down kingdom of Jesus, "danger" is actually a really good thing, a life-changing thing, a hold-on-to-your-hats-because-this-is-going-to-be-a-wild-ride thing. So welcome to the anything-but-safe book of Acts! But you know what else this Bible study is? Fun. Adventurous. Riveting.

We don't know what you've heard about Acts, but we're guessing you at least know it has something to do with the beginning of the church and a lot to do with the Holy Spirit. Maybe you've heard some stuff about Paul, Pentecost, or perhaps "tongues of fire"!

Some of you are probably eager to jump into this study so you can finally figure out what your spiritual gift is. (Is it prophecy, healing, words of wisdom, speaking in tongues?) You can't wait to be inspired by the apostles and start evangelizing to the ends of the earth. Others of you are probably freaked out wondering if we're going to ask you to start translating tongues by chapter 3. (Spoiler alert—*we're not!*)

No matter what you're feeling right now or what you know about the book of Acts, we want to prepare you for what lies ahead. We weren't kidding when we said Acts isn't safe. It's inevitably dangerous in nature, so your choice to study it is a risky one. And it will be hard.

Now, you might be wondering, *But why is it risky and hard? After all, I thought this was just a Bible study!*

You see, all throughout this study we're talking about the Holy Spirit. And if there's one thing we know to be true, it's that although walking with the Holy Spirit can be fun, adventurous, and full of the miraculous, it can also be inconvenient, uncomfortable, and unpredictable. Throughout the book of Acts you'll see that during their adventure with the Holy Spirit, the apostles ended up in some really tough situations. They were imprisoned, shipwrecked, bitten by snakes, stoned—some were even martyred for their faith in Jesus. (Need we remind you that the Spirit led even Jesus himself into the wilderness to be tempted by the enemy? Don't believe us? Read Matthew 4:1.)

Now, we don't think such an extreme will be experienced by the majority of us, but we do believe the journey won't be easy. It will take bold courage and trust in the face of adversity. That's what we mean when we say this adventure will be *hard and dangerous*.

And we're not just going to read about the Spirit. We're inviting the Spirit to *fill* us, together making the decision that a life lived with Him is ten times more worthwhile than a life lived without Him. So be prepared for the unexpected. Be prepared to be inconvenienced. Be prepared to have your world turned upside down as we invite the Holy Spirit to come and do in our lives what He did in the early church and what He continues to do all around us.

HOW TO USE THIS STUDY

This is a seven-week study designed for you to dive *deep* into Scripture. And we'll be reading the *entire* book of Acts, verse by verse. Technically, you'll have four days of content for each week, but you can set your own pace because there's quite a bit of reading and studying to get through each day. Some days' content might take you longer, so split it all up however you like. But be sure to leave yourself the space to pause and process rather than charge through just to check off another day.

Taking an Interactive Approach

You'll see these four interactive elements throughout this study:

1. **STOP AND READ**—This is your cue to slowly read through the Scripture for yourself. We hope you don't mind marking in your Bible, because we encourage you to highlight what stands out, circle things you think are important, and jot down notes in the margins. But use a journal for all this if you prefer. We so believe in engaging with Scripture as much as possible. The words you read in your Bible will be far more important than the words you read in this book. We don't want you to miss them!
2. **FILL IN THE BLANKS**—This is where we ask you to complete a Scripture verse or passage by filling in the blanks we've provided. Why? To help what you read really sink in. The Bible translation we use for this and all Scripture quotations is the NIV. If you don't have a copy of an NIV Bible, you can find it online to help you accurately fill in the blanks.
3. **TAKE NOTE**—These questions simply ask you to review, especially notice, or consider something specific in the Scripture you just read and write it down.
4. **REFLECT ON THIS**—This is your opportunity to reflect on the text and process what you're reading, usually by answering a question or two in writing. Be sure you're being honest and real, not just skimming the surface. These questions are there to help you stay engaged with the text and give you the space to sit with God and let Him search your heart.

Experiencing This Adventure *Together*!

We're so excited for you to dive right in, immerse yourself in Scripture, get honest with yourself, and experience the Holy Spirit. But although you'll do some of that on your own, you won't be alone, because we're also going on this adventure *together*.

For Kenz's bachelorette party a few years ago, we went white water rafting in Wyoming. It was one of the more hilarious experiences of our lives. Just picture eight girls clueless as to what they were doing, screaming in an inflatable boat, rushing down a ridiculously intense river.

If you know anything about white water rafting, then you probably know it's typically accomplished in a four-to-ten-person raft led by a guide. The lightest people usually sit in the front of the raft so it doesn't take an unexpected nosedive on a rapid. And most agree that the front happens to be the spot that gets the wettest and sees the most action. Guess who got the coveted spot in the front of our raft. You guessed it! *The five-foot-two bride-to-be, Kenz!*

As we got started on our excursion, the rapids were easy, and our river guide steered the raft while also instructing us when to paddle and when to wait. Adrenaline began pumping through our bodies as we made it through several difficult rapids with no major spills or faux pas.

But then we saw it. We'd rounded a bend in the river, and up ahead lay the most terrifying stretch of water we'd ever seen. It was solid white water for as far as the eye could see, ending with a huge downward drop. We watched as one of the rafts ahead of us capsized and three passengers were tossed into the river with only their life preservers keeping them afloat. Over the sound of the rapids, our guide screamed at us, "Paddle forward!" There was no turning back!

While without a doubt this white water rafting experience was anything but safe, it was one of the best adventures we've ever been on together. We still reminisce about it to this day! And just like we took a dangerous but thrilling white water rafting trip in Wyoming, we're about to go on this anything-but-safe adventure through Acts with you. We can't wait!

We're *soooo* excited, honored, and humbled to be your human "guides" on this journey. We'll be at the back steering the whole way through, telling you when to paddle harder through the tougher parts and letting you know when to simply sit, wait, and listen as the Spirit truly guides us. But you'll be in the front seat because we want you to experience the fullness of this journey. (Remember, this is where you'll get the most wet!) Hopefully, half the time you'll forget we're behind you, and you'll see only the wild and beautiful Spirit of God ahead of you, beneath you, and all around you.

But anytime fear starts to creep its way in, or the water ahead seems rougher than you imagined it would be, just look behind you. We'll be there, because, again, this is an adventure we're taking together—you, us, and hopefully thousands of other women who choose the goodness of God over the safe, life with the Spirit over the ordinary, and adventure over control.

OK, are you ready to paddle forward? Let's do this, *together*.

XOXO,
Mac & Kenz

Taking It a Step Further on Our *For The Girl* Podcast

If you want to get even more out of this study, listen to or watch all seven coinciding episodes on the podcast we host, *For The Girl* (ForTheGirl.com/podcast). You'll find it wherever you get your podcasts.

Actually, are you looking for your new favorite podcast that's both entertaining and challenging in your walk with Jesus—no matter what your stage of life? *For the Girl* might be it. Every Tuesday we break down things we wish someone had told us in our twenties. From faith and relationships to wild career transitions, we get real about all our missteps and what God has taught us along the way. Tune in to take deep dives into Scripture, follow chitchats with Mac and Kenz about each topic, and learn tangible ways you can experience the Spirit in your day-to-day life.

Supporting Group Leaders

This is a perfect Bible study for any small group. It's great for women of all ages and can create incredible conversations across all generations. But groups need leaders.

First things first: Head to ForTheGirl.com to sign up to lead a group and you'll gain access to our For The Girl Group Leader Portal. There, we share all our best tips and tricks on how to gather a group of women and lead them through one of our studies.

At the end of each week's content, we've provided a Group Guide we hope is a simple and easy way to facilitate powerful conversation for your community. Each group time is split into three parts:

1. Discuss and Reflect.

For the first part of your time together, review what you read in your individual study time. As the leader, you can summarize the Scripture and pull out some of your favorite verses, quotes, or key points. Ask the questions provided to spark conversation and get the convo rolling.

2. Let's Get Real.

True Christ-centered community involves confession and vulnerability within a trusted circle. This is your chance to invite your group to get real about how they're struggling and how the Holy Spirit convicted or challenged them that week. As the leader, be willing to go first. Lead with vulnerability by sharing your raw and real struggles. Fight against the pressure to be "perfect" just because you're the leader. When we're vulnerable and real, it allows other people to be vulnerable in return. It quite literally breaks chains!

Also, be sure to get super comfortable with silence in this part of your session. Sometimes people need some extra time to open up. You don't want to shut off the conversation before they're ready to speak up and share.

3. Put It into Action.

This is where head knowledge transforms into powerful spiritual experience. Each week you'll go through a different Holy Spirit–focused activity designed to help each person practically engage with the truths you're reading about in Acts. These activities create space for people to experience God's presence together rather than only *talking* about Him.

As the leader, participate fully and model openness to what the Spirit might do. Some weeks may feel uncomfortable or new for certain group members, but that's OK! Encourage participation at members' own comfort level while gently inviting them to stretch their faith. The book of Acts shows us a Spirit-empowered church in action, and these activities will help people begin to walk in that same power and presence in their everyday lives.

For more tips on leading Bible study groups, check out our website, ForTheGirl.com, for all our best tips.

ACTS 1–2

Mac

week one: day 1

The Who, What, and Why Behind Acts

Acts 1

Welcome to our first week of studying together! Kenz and I are so excited about digging into the book of Acts with you. This week we're covering the first and second chapters of Acts, and trust me when I say we have a *lot* to discuss.

The book of Acts picks up where the Gospels of Matthew, Mark, Luke, and John leave off. This is what unfolds after the crucifixion and resurrection of Jesus. It lays out the story of the very first church, and we'll get a beautiful look into the lives of the men and women who were the very first to spread the good news of the gospel of Jesus. This is what follows Easter! After the egg hunts are over and the pastel dresses are put away, what happens next? Some wildly cool things I can't wait to dig into!

I'm not going to waste our time with a cute and witty introduction to draw your attention. I promise the Scripture speaks for itself. Instead, I'll ask you to pull out your Bible, pen, highlighter, journal, and whatever else you like to use to study the Word.

We'll start with Acts 1:1: "In my former book, Theophilus . . ."

OK, hold up! We're five words in and there's already *soooo* much to talk about! First up, the author says, "In my former book"? This is important. The book of Acts is actually the sequel to a book we know and love: the gospel of Luke. We can't miss this when reading the book of Acts. Imagine suggesting that someone should watch your most beloved Netflix show and later finding out they started on season 2. You'd probably be appalled because you know season 2 doesn't really make sense without the context of season 1.

In the same way, the book of Acts makes more sense in light of the book of Luke. Many scholars think of these separate books as one piece of writing by referring to them as "Luke–Acts" because they're believed to be written by the same author—Luke. They're powerful as separate entities, but trust me when I say they're even more life-changing when you understand them together. So we'll do our best to point out their connections, repetitions, and similarities as we study together, but we also suggest taking some time to refresh your memory on Luke as we continue our journey.

To recap: Acts is a follow-up to the book of Luke, one of the four Gospels. *But who is this guy Luke?* Luke is thought to have been a beloved traveling physician, friend, and companion to the apostle Paul, whom we'll get to know very well in this study. Luke even subtly inserts himself into the story of Acts when he writes with first-person pronouns *we*, *our*, and *us* to describe some of Paul's missionary journeys. Luke was, without a doubt, an eyewitness to the early days of the church. It makes sense that he was the one to record this story in such great detail! (*Side note:* Paul gave Luke a shout-out in his letter to the church at Colossae. Flip over to Colossians 4:14 to see for yourself.)

So we know the gospel writer Luke is the author of the book of Acts, and in verse 1 we find out who he was writing to: *Theophilus*. And guess what. The book of Luke happens to be addressed to Theophilus too.

STOP AND READ: Luke 1:1–3

FILL IN THE BLANKS: Luke 1:3

> I too decided to write an orderly account for you,
>
> _______________ _______________ _______________.

But who was this Theophilus guy, anyway? Luke referred to him as "most excellent," a term used to address people who held a high political office.[1] Whoever he was, Luke thought he was pretty important! After all, Luke spent a lot of time writing two extremely long letters to him.

Biblical scholars aren't sure whether Luke was writing to a specific person named Theophilus or he chose a symbolic name to represent a wider audience. But we do know Theophilus means "God-lover" or "lover of God."[2] So it's possible that Luke was writing to a man named Theophilus, but maybe, just maybe, he was actually writing to people who identified as lovers of God. And that might even include *you and me*. I think this right here is our invitation into the beautiful story of Acts!

I don't know where you are currently on your journey with God. Maybe it's been a while since you've read your Bible, maybe your heart is more on fire than ever, or perhaps this is the first time you've ever tried to give this whole "Jesus thing" a go. But wherever you are, do some reflecting right now.

REFLECT ON THIS: Where do you currently stand with God? How does your heart feel toward Him these days?

Again, I don't know where you find yourself with God right now, but since you're taking time for this study, I assume you have some interest in going deeper with Him. And maybe some part of you identifies as a lover of God. But wherever you are, every word in Acts is meant for you to read, study, and absorb. I believe if we yield our hearts to its story, we'll see so much transformation in our lives!

OK! Time to review. So far, we've learned at least two things together: who wrote the book of Acts and who the intended audience was.

So now that we've gathered some context about Luke, let's answer another question: *Why* did he write it?

A *lot* of people *way* smarter than me have a *lot* of theories about Luke's reasons for writing Acts, but I want to focus on one idea I find really convincing. Luke himself hinted at it in the first few verses, starting with verse 1 (emphasis mine): "In my former book, Theophilus, *I wrote about all that Jesus began to do and to teach.*"

The book of Luke was written as a record of what Jesus did and taught. We already know Acts is the sequel to Luke, so we can confidently conclude that Acts is the *continuation of this story*.

The book of Acts is often referred to as The Acts of the Apostles, but a more accurate name could be The Acts of Jesus and the Spirit. Although Jesus is physically present during only the first nine verses, He remains the primary and unifying character in Acts even after He physically departs from the story.

This is why we can assume that Acts is the continuation of what Jesus did and taught through the power of the Holy Spirit in the lives of the ordinary men and women who would come to be known as the early church. So ultimately, Luke wrote the book of Acts *to tell us more about Jesus!* Jesus is the lens through which we'll read this entire story.

Wow! That's a lot of information about only the first verse of Acts. I promise we'll start moving more quickly as we keep studying, but this context will be incredibly relevant as we dive further into this fascinating and life-changing story. File it away, and let's keep reading!

STOP AND READ: Acts 1:1–3

TAKE NOTE: In what period of time did Jesus appear to the disciples (1:3), and what did He speak about (1:3)?

The book of Acts begins by giving us an update on what happened after the resurrection of Jesus. If you remember from the book of Luke, Jesus had just been crucified, lain dead in a tomb for three days, and miraculously come back to life (aka resurrected). After all that chaos, the disciples hung out with the risen Jesus for several weeks—forty days to be exact. During that time, Jesus continued teaching them all about the upside-down kingdom of God.

The number forty might ring a bell when it comes to the Bible. It's an incredibly significant number that often implies a period of testing or trial mentioned close to 150 times throughout the pages of Scripture. Here are some of the instances you'll probably remember:

- God flooded the earth during the time of Noah. It rained for forty days and forty nights.
- The Israelites wandered in the wilderness for forty years before they were allowed to enter the promised land.
- Moses lived in exile for forty years before he encountered God at the burning bush, and God called him to free the Israelite people from Pharaoh.
- Jesus was tempted in the wilderness for forty days before He began His ministry.

I can't help but wonder if those forty days the disciples spent with Jesus ever felt like a testing or trial of the validity of the resurrection. I'm guessing there were a lot of whispers behind Jesus's back, as well as some doubters like the disciple Thomas. But Jesus resurrected exactly like He'd promised He would, and that changed *everything*.

TAKE NOTE: What were some things Jesus told the disciples and His other followers in those forty days? See:

- John 20:16–17

- John 20:21–23

- Matthew 28:18-20

- Luke 24:44-49

- John 21:15-19

After His resurrection, Jesus reminded the disciples about so many of the things He taught before His death. But after the events that had just occurred in Jerusalem, those messages took on new layers of meaning for the disciples. Those messages about peace, believing without physical proof, the kingdom of God, Jesus being the fulfillment of prophecy, and the Holy Spirit all meant something more as the disciples began to understand Jesus's teachings in a new way—in light of the resurrection.

You see, everything changed *in light of the resurrection!*

I know the same to be true in my life. Everything changed for me when I truly began to understand what Jesus did for me on that cross and that He didn't stay in the grave but resurrected exactly as He said He would. This wasn't necessarily a head knowledge moment but rather a beautiful heart knowledge moment when I felt overwhelmed by the love of Jesus and His choosing to make a way of rescue for me.

Before we read another verse in Acts, I think it's so important for each of us to simply reflect on how we're different because of the resurrection! More head knowledge about Scripture is great, but it pales in comparison to the heart knowledge of who Jesus is in your life and how He beautifully rescued you.

To close out today, I encourage you to spend time with Jesus, reflecting on His rescuing love for you. How are you different because of knowing Him? How do you want to know Him more? What are you hoping to get out of this study in the weeks to come?

week one: day 2

God's Plan A

Acts 1

We're back! And I promise we'll read a lot more than three verses today. After all, we have twenty-eight chapters to get through in seven weeks.

The passage we're looking at today is packed with so much I can't wait to dig into it, so let's just jump right in!

STOP AND READ: Acts 1:4–11

In verse 4 of Acts 1, the disciples gather for a meal with Jesus. We can imagine they were amped up, ready for Jesus's blessing to go tell the world about God's new kingdom and the resurrection. But Jesus did something else instead.

TAKE NOTE: What did Jesus tell the disciples to do (1:4)?

That's right—Jesus told the disciples to *wait*.

Wait? Are you kidding me? The extroverts are squirming in their seats right now! Jesus gave the disciples clear instructions to *wait* until they received the

Holy Spirit before they set forth on the mission He'd given them. But Jesus knew something that was extremely important: Their effectiveness in the kingdom of God depended on the power of the Spirit in their lives.

REFLECT ON THIS: How often do you wait for the Spirit to move before *you* move?

If you're like Kenz and me, you might be saying to yourself, *Um, ouch!* The hard truth is that in our twenty-first-century kingdom, we really stink at waiting. Waiting isn't exactly cute and sexy! Waiting is an act of submission to God's plan, will, and timeline. This sounds all spiritual and great, but let's be honest, it's not exactly fun or exhilarating. Waiting in the kingdom of God means surrendering control, recognizing that you must wait to receive something better than what you could create for yourself.

Again, ouch!

Waiting isn't convenient, but many of us have personally experienced how waiting on the Spirit to move is actually super worth it. The disciples were itching to begin their journeys, but Jesus knew *this* would definitely be worth the wait. They were going to be baptized by the Holy Spirit!

But they clearly didn't know the full implications of what Jesus said, so they followed up with a question.

FILL IN THE BLANKS: Acts 1:6

> Then they gathered around him and ____________ him, "Lord, are you at this time going to ____________ the kingdom to Israel?"

They wanted to know if the Israelite people would finally be restored to power. Their ancestors had lived under the political reign of King David and King Solomon, but the disciples lived under the oppression of the Roman Empire. Old Testament prophecies gave them hope to cling to in dark times, with talk of a spiritual and national rebirth of Israel in the ages to come. They interpreted the resurrection of Jesus as a spiritual rebirth, and they wanted to know if a national rebirth of Israel was on the horizon too. Was life about to return to the way it had been in the days of their ancestors?

I love how Jesus responded. He told the disciples they weren't allowed to know the exact time and date, but then He promised them two things.

TAKE NOTE: What two things does Jesus promise (Acts 1:8)?

Jesus promised the disciples, **"You will receive power."** The disciples were going to receive power through the Holy Spirit! Jesus didn't give them the result they wanted (the immediate restoration of Israel), but He gave them power to achieve spiritual restoration in Israel.

Even though these words were spoken so long ago and far outside of our context, I believe they transcend time and remain incredibly relevant to our current situation.

Let's be honest. We live in a world riddled with brokenness, sickness, racism, hatred, prejudice, and inequality—to name a few. I don't know if you've turned on the news recently or scrolled through your social media feeds, but it often feels like our world is falling apart at the seams. People are shouting out to God, desperate for answers: *When will You redeem this world, God? When will You solve our problems? When will You fix our brokenness?*

I imagine God looking at His beloved children and responding to us with words eerily similar to what Jesus said to the disciples before His ascension (paraphrased): "The timing of My work is not for you to know. But here's what you can know: You already have the power within you to get the result you want."

Through the death and resurrection of Jesus, God has equipped us with the power of the Holy Spirit to face the brokenness of our world head-on. We are God's plan A for the world!

How can we respond to the issues of mental illness plaguing generations? By harnessing the strength of the Holy Spirit to guide us in hard conversations, shine light in the places of darkness the enemy has tried to control, and carry the burdens of people who are slowly losing hope, lifting them up to Jesus.

How can we come together in the midst of intense political polarization? By harnessing the goodness of the Holy Spirit to unify around one common enemy—evil—and one common mission—bringing the kingdom of God to earth as it is in heaven.

How can we work to end racism and prejudice in our world? By harnessing the power of the Holy Spirit in our hearts to listen well, empathize, mourn, and boldly pursue change, justice, and action in our spheres of influence.

I know these might sound like incomplete, quick fixes to centuries-old issues, but if we believe in the almighty power of our God, then we have to start believing in the almighty power of His redemption plan. God sent His Son to die on the cross and rise again, and—I'll say it again—that changed *everything*! Then He left His story and legacy in the hands of incapable, unimpressive men and women (like us), who were given the power of the Holy Spirit to be witnesses of His love to the ends of the earth.

We might feel overwhelmed by the chaos around us, but the plan hasn't changed! *We are God's plan A for a broken world.*

REFLECT ON THIS: How does being a part of God's plan A challenge you?

What brokenness in the world do you sense God calling you to face head on with His Spirit?

His second promise was "**You will be my witnesses.**" What was the result of the power Jesus promised? The disciples would become eyewitnesses to the resurrection, truth, and mission of Jesus in their hometowns, the neighboring cities, and the nations. It wasn't a command; it was a declaration: "You *will* receive God's power, and you *will* be My witnesses."

You want to know what I love most about God's plan A? When we walk in the power of the Holy Spirit, we don't get the fame and attention, Jesus does! *Jesus gets the glory.* His is the name that's remembered, honored, and praised.

But many of us have it backward. We do good things in the name of Jesus, but if we're honest, we have to admit we often want the glory for ourselves. We'll know we're truly walking in the power of the Spirit when other people come to know the source of that power rather than the person walking in it. When we follow God's plan, we have the power to achieve the results we want (healing, peace, restoration, redemption, rest, joy), Jesus gets more famous, and heaven gets a lot more crowded.

That's good news!

REFLECT ON THIS: Have you been working for your own glory? How so?

What would it look like to truly let your good deeds, gifts, and praise point back to Jesus?

Whatever issues are plaguing your world, remember that you're a part of God's redemption plan. Wait on the Spirit to move, walk boldly in His power, and give God the glory when He does what only *He* can do.

Acts 1:8 gives us a spoiler alert for the remainder of the book. Just like Jesus promised, the Holy Spirit came to the disciples, and the people of God were unleashed as witnesses in Jerusalem, Judea, Samaria, and beyond.

Jesus finished His final conversation with the disciples and ascended into heaven in a cloud (v. 9). In the Bible, clouds often represent the powerful presence of God. I like to imagine God's arms reaching down, enveloping Jesus in a proud fatherly hug, and inviting Him to join the exuberant welcome home party in heaven after a job well done.

After the ascension of Jesus, the disciples stared in awe at the sky. Out of nowhere, two angels appeared to bring some clarity to the situation (v. 10). They looked at the disciples and asked an important question.

STOP AND READ: Acts 1:11–14

TAKE NOTE: What question do the angels ask the disciples, and what do the angels tell them about Jesus (1:11)?

Verse 12 gives us a glimpse into the disciples' next steps, and this gets me hype!: "Then the apostles returned to Jerusalem from the hill called the Mount of Olives, a Sabbath day's walk from the city."

The disciples *returned to Jerusalem!*

If you're unimpressed and underwhelmed right now because you think I'm crazy to believe walking for a whole day is cool, remember what Jesus had told these guys to do just a few verses earlier.

FILL IN THE BLANKS: Acts 1:4

> On one occasion, while he was eating with them, he gave them this command: "Do not leave ____________________, but wait for the ____________________ my Father promised, which you have heard me speak about."

Jesus told the disciples to stay in Jerusalem and wait. So what did they do? *They returned to Jerusalem and waited.* The disciples responded in *obedience*. It might seem elementary, but walking in obedience is a discipline that so many followers of Jesus, including me, struggle to do well. But the disciples had been in fellowship with the risen Jesus for forty days, and their encounter compelled them to obedient action.

Continue reading to see what they did next. It keeps getting better!

TAKE NOTE: What does verse 14 tell us the disciples did together?

They prayed! The eleven apostles (we'll get to what happened to the twelfth shortly); Jesus's mother, Mary; Jesus's brothers; and the women who had traveled with Jesus during His ministry all met in Jerusalem and prayed together.

First off, they were *joined together*. If you remember from the Gospels, the disciples were a classic dysfunctional family that bickered and disagreed often. But just forty days later, they were getting along swimmingly. Scripture tells us they were joined together constantly in prayer. I imagine their hearts were on fire for the resurrected Jesus as they held tightly to the words He'd left them with. Remember, He told them to *wait*! So they gathered together, united in prayer, actively waited, and interceded day and night, asking God to make His next move.

This brief passage teaches me so much about what it looks like to wait on the Spirit to move. We don't do it by scrolling through Instagram or binge-watching shows on Netflix—we wait on our knees. We wait through intercession. We wait by uniting in communal prayer. We wait by obeying what Jesus has already asked us to do.

Don't you wish you could've been a fly on the wall during those sacred days before the arrival of the Holy Spirit? I can imagine songs of praise mixed with shouts of hope and cries of desperation floating through the atmosphere day and night. Although they had to wait, the disciples waited well.

REFLECT ON THIS: When you're waiting, how often do you turn to prayer?

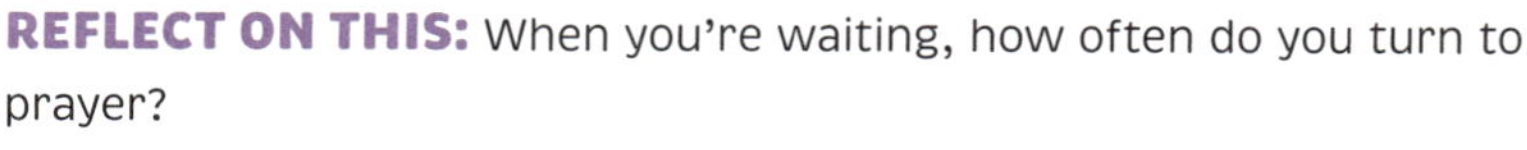

What are you currently waiting on?

How have you been using your season of waiting?

What might you need to change to wait well?

Before I ask you to read the rest of Acts 1 on your own, let me comment on what you'll read.

As the disciples waited, they had some administrative work to take care of. Judas, one of the twelve disciples and the one who ultimately betrayed Jesus, was no longer alive, and they needed to find a replacement for him. They used a method called "casting lots," which is essentially like rolling dice or flipping a coin and trusting that God would be in that decision-making process. At the time, this was their best way of relying on God. Remember, this was *before* the arrival of the Holy Spirit. The author Luke gives us contrast between what once was and what was about to be.

How wild that in just a few short days the Holy Spirit would be living inside all of them, guiding their every step. Now that I think about it, that's a beautiful thing to wait for! How fun is it to see God's plan A beginning to unfold in the world?

STOP AND READ: Now read Acts 1:15–26 (Take notes on anything that stands out to you.)

week one: day 3

The Power of the Spirit

Acts 2

Just like that, we're back for Day 3 of our dangerous and exciting study of the book of Acts. As we closed out Acts 1 yesterday, we left the disciples expectantly waiting in obedience, community, and prayer for Jesus's promises to be fulfilled. Today we're picking up the story in Acts 2.

Let me go ahead and warn you: This portion of Scripture will be action-packed! Today and tomorrow we'll journey through forty-seven verses of outrageous, *amazing* events.

FILL IN THE BLANKS: Acts 2:1-2

> When the day of ____________________ came, they were all together in one place. Suddenly a sound like the blowing of a violent ____________________ came from heaven and filled the whole house where they were sitting.

It's Pentecost in Jerusalem! Keep in mind that just fifty-ish days earlier, Jesus had entered Jerusalem on a donkey to celebrate the Passover festival. Jewish festivals were a big deal in the ancient world. It was during Passover that Jesus was arrested, crucified, and resurrected. If you haven't noticed,

God is *super* intentional, so the fact that all this took place during Passover wasn't random—it symbolized the connection between past and present.

Need a memory jog about the significance of Passover?

STOP AND READ: Flip over to Exodus 11 and read verses 1–10.

Think back to Exodus chapters 7–11 when God sent plagues to Egypt so Pharaoh would free the Israelites from slavery. The tenth and final plague, which ultimately led to Israel's freedom, was the death of the firstborn son of every household, including Pharaoh's. But Moses and Aaron relayed God's message to the Hebrew people: If they sacrificed a lamb and painted its blood over the entrance of their home, the plague would "pass over" their household and spare their sons.

Jesus is the tangible and symbolic Passover Lamb, whom God sacrificed to save us all. The story of Passover points to the story of Jesus!

Guess what. In the same way, Pentecost also points to Jesus. In the Old Testament, the Jewish feast of Pentecost (called Shavuot) was held in honor of the firstfruits of the wheat harvest.[1] Jewish pilgrims from all over the region and world would gather in Jerusalem to feast, celebrate, and offer the firstfruits of their harvests to God. Bible scholar R. Kent Hughes mentions that this would have been the best attended festival of the year due to optimal travel conditions.[2]

This was *a big deal* in the Holy City! The streets were busier than ever, alive and abuzz with beautifully diverse commotion, and everyone's long-lost relatives were in town. Now that the scene is set, we're about to witness the celebration of firstfruits from a new, spiritual harvest.

STOP AND READ: Acts 2:1–13

TAKE NOTE: What happened in Acts 2:2?

Acts 2:2 tells us "a violent wind came from heaven" and entered into the house where the disciples were staying. This heavenly wind swept through the room, bringing with it a blaze that splintered off into tongues of fire that hovered over each person. Verse 4 says they were "filled with the Holy Spirit" and began speaking in other languages, enabled by the Spirit. This is what the disciples had waited for! We're seeing the firstfruits of the Holy Spirit and the beginning of the early church.

The scene we're watching unfold is incredibly significant. In Day 2, I mentioned that in the Bible, clouds often signified God's presence. Fire is another common symbol used throughout Scripture to indicate the powerful presence of God.

If you flip back to the Old Testament book of Exodus, you'll see how God's presence showed up through fire on Mount Sinai when He gave His people the Ten Commandments (Exodus 19–20). Other parts of the Exodus story tell us that God's presence traveled with the Israelites through a single pillar of fire at night.

In Acts, Luke makes an important distinction between these images. Instead of one huge pillar of fire like in Exodus, this time we see *individual* tongues of fire, resting over each and every person gathered in the house.

God's presence moved from the *old* temple into the *new* temple, the body of Jesus—aka His people and His church. Wow! This meant the Spirit of God didn't just live *beside* His people but dwelled *within* them. This changed everything! The promise that Jesus made just ten days earlier had come to fruition. The people of God finally received the gift of the Holy Spirit.

Right away, the people who received this new power began declaring the wonders of God, but they were speaking in languages that just ten minutes earlier they hadn't known. People who had traveled from all over the ancient world to be in Jerusalem for the festival gathered in awe as they heard the story of Jesus told in their native tongues for the first time.

TAKE NOTE: How did some people respond to this moment in 2:12, and how did others respond in 2:13?

From the beginning of time, people have responded to the power of God in different ways. Verse 12 tells us some were "amazed and perplexed." These people leaned in closer, eager to understand what all this meant. But as we see in verse 13, others wrote it all off as the result of drunkenness. (LOL! I mean, Jesus *did* have a reputation for turning water into wine.)

REFLECT ON THIS: Let's get honest. How have you typically responded when you've witnessed the Holy Spirit move?

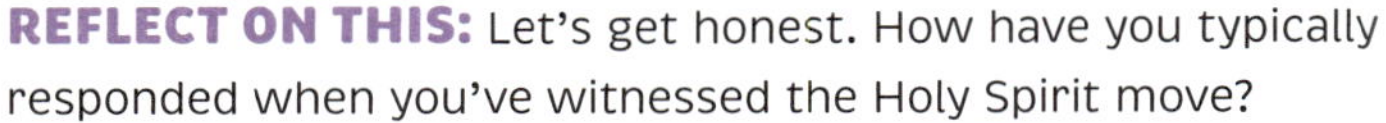

Think about a time you saw the Spirit move. Why do you think you responded the way you did? *(Totally OK if you can't think of a time!)*

Has anything affected or tainted the way you've personally experienced the Spirit? If so, what was it?

The Spirit of God is beautifully perplexing, comforting, and sometimes disturbing all at the same time. When the Spirit moves, the people of God are called to move too. We're invited into the story as active participants, not sideline dwellers.

FILL IN THE BLANK: Acts 2:4

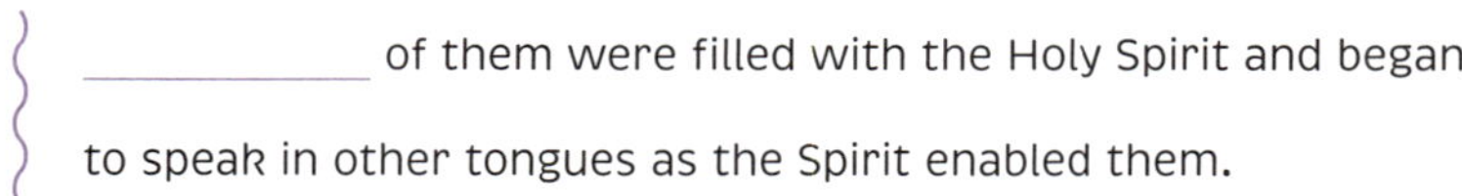

____________ of them were filled with the Holy Spirit and began to speak in other tongues as the Spirit enabled them.

Notice that Luke said the Spirit fell on *all* of them. The Holy Spirit fell on every single person in that room that day. It didn't skip over the person nervously sitting in the corner, it didn't move past the person who had just joined the group the day before, and it didn't avoid the person who felt like an outsider. The Holy Spirit fell on everybody present.

So my questions to all of us are

- Who are we to exclude ourselves from the power of the Holy Spirit resting in us? Who are we to disqualify ourselves?
- Who are we to say the Spirit is reserved for the religious elite or charismatic churches?
- Who are we to exclude somebody else from the power of the Holy Spirit resting on them?
- Who are we to turn access to God into an exclusive club or hierarchy?
- Who are we to decide who's "spiritual enough" and who isn't?

The Spirit is for *all* of us. For you, your family, your friends, your neighbors, and even your enemies. For young and old; black, brown, and white; male and female; rich, middle class, and poor; "spiritual" and "unspiritual." Jesus sent His Spirit for every single person who knows Him and loves Him. That's the only invitation we need to live a life filled with the Spirit!

The disciples in that room needed only a relationship with Jesus for complete, total, easy access to the power of the Spirit. There was no limit based on career choice, church background, education, theological beliefs, or personality type. *It was simply about who they knew!* They knew Jesus, they'd walked with Jesus, they'd been transformed by Jesus—and *that* was all they needed.

Regardless of your experiences with the Holy Spirit in the past, this is an opportunity to put aside your preconceived notions, biases, and fears and start afresh. Just as the Spirit fell on the early church for the first time, let the Spirit fall afresh on you right here and right now. Let a heavenly wind sweep through your heart and awaken the parts of your soul that have perhaps gone numb to the power of God.

REFLECT ON THIS: Pray right now, asking the Holy Spirit to fall afresh on you. Then write down whatever the Spirit of God brings into your heart. *(There are no right or wrong answers here!)*

week one: day 4

A Story Redeemed

Acts 2

I hope you're still glowing from your moment with the Holy Spirit yesterday. *I know I am!* We're about to wrap up our first week in Acts, and I'm just in awe of all we've already learned and experienced together. The Bible is pretty incredible, right?

Let's move on and start by reading just one verse: Acts 2:14. An incredible moment of transformation and redemption is about to unfold before our very eyes.

STOP AND READ: Acts 2:14

TAKE NOTE: Who addressed the crowd in Acts 2:14?

Peter stood in front of the crowd and delivered a passionate, powerful message about what was unfolding at Pentecost. But this was so much more than a three-point sermon! Acts 2 details a total redemptive transformation of our friend Peter. So let's dig into his past so we can fully understand the magnitude of what's happening here.

STOP AND READ: Flip back to Luke 5 and skim through verses 1-11.

In this passage, you see the moment when Jesus first approached Peter (who at the time was called Simon) and his brother on the beach of the Sea of Galilee. Jesus asked to borrow their boat to speak to a crowd, and after delivering His message, He told Simon to cast his fishing nets back into the water. Simon scoffed and told Jesus it was pointless—they hadn't caught a thing all night. But Simon relented, and he caught so many fish that the boat started sinking.

After this miraculous event, Jesus called Simon to leave the fishing nets behind, follow Him, and become a "fisher of men."

STOP AND READ: Head to Matthew 16 and skim through verses 13-20.

Here we see that Jesus took the disciples to Caesarea Philippi, an area north of Galilee. Jesus asked them who they believed Him to be. Simon boldly spoke up and said, "You are the Messiah, the Son of the living God" (16:16).

He wasn't just a rabbi, a prophet, or a great teacher; He was the Son of God. Jesus responded to this truth by renaming Simon as Peter, Greek for "stone" or "rock." Jesus told Peter He would build His church "on this rock" (16:18)—in other words, on the reality of Peter's declaration that He was the Son of God. (Whoa!)

STOP AND READ: Next, skim through Luke 22:54-62.

TAKE NOTE: What does Peter do three times?

Peter did the thing he swore he would never do—deny Jesus. And he did it out of fear, not once but three times! Peter, heartbroken, wept at how quickly his heart was led astray from his deep love for Jesus.

STOP AND READ: Now turn to John 21 and skim through verses 1-19.

In this passage, Jesus had been crucified and the disciples were back in Galilee. Peter suggested they return to fishing, but they didn't catch anything. A man from the beach suggested they throw their net on the other side of the boat. After they did, their nets came up completely full! At that moment Peter realized who was standing on the beach—Jesus. He leapt out of the boat and ran to embrace the risen Son of God. We can imagine that while Peter was elated to be with Jesus again, the shame and disappointment of his denial of Jesus likely weighed heavily on his spirit.

While they shared a meal, Jesus looked at Peter and asked a simple question: "Do you love me?" (21:15). Peter responded that of course he did. In the same verse, Jesus responded, "Feed my lambs." This exchange happened three times total, with Jesus asking Peter to then care for and, again, feed His lambs, covering Peter's three denials from a few days earlier.

I love this! Peter's mistake didn't affect his usefulness or calling in the kingdom of God. Jesus still used Peter to build His church. That's why Acts 2:14 is so monumental—we're seeing the promise of Jesus come to fruition. Peter's spirit was transformed by grace, from timid denial to bold proclamation.

FILL IN THE BLANKS: Acts 2:14

> Then Peter stood up with the Eleven, ______________
>
> ______________ ______________ and addressed the crowd: "Fellow
>
> Jews and all of you who live in Jerusalem, let me explain this to
>
> you; listen carefully to what I say."

Luke tells us Peter raised his voice. He had newfound courage and boldness that stood in stark contrast to his three denials of Jesus just a few weeks prior. Peter was filled with the Holy Spirit and began to spontaneously preach with authority, calling the people gathered there to repent and be baptized in the name of Jesus.

This gives my heart such hope! My guess is that some of you feel as though your past or your sins have canceled your usefulness in the kingdom of God. At times, that has felt true in my own life. To be honest, I've screwed up too many times to count. I've chosen the easy way rather than the faithful way, and like Peter, I've even denied my love for Jesus. The enemy often wants us to believe that when we mess up, we're disqualified from God's kingdom. We fall victim to the lie that we have to clean ourselves off before coming to the arms of Jesus.

But because of what Jesus did on the cross, we get to approach the throne with all our screw-ups, regrets, and messes. Jesus does the cleaning up, the sifting through, and the redeeming. He takes our broken pieces and makes us into new vessels that can be used to carry His goodness into the world. We see firsthand evidence of that through the life of Peter!

Your mistakes don't cancel out your worth and value. Rather, they're invitations to draw closer to Jesus and experience grace-filled transformation. I have to believe that Peter's story is so much like many of ours!

REFLECT ON THIS: Do you feel that anything in your life or a decision from your past has canceled your usefulness in the kingdom? What is it?

Are you ready to let it go or at least leave it behind?

No matter where you find yourself on this scale, write out a prayer asking Jesus to redeem the broken pieces of your life for His good. Like Peter did, allow Him to give you a new vision for your purpose in His kingdom.

Back to Peter's message. What exactly did he stand up and say at Pentecost? *A lot!* To close out today, after reading Acts 2:14–47 on your own, check out the next three bullet points to gain a deeper understanding of all that Peter preached on that day.

I can't wait to be back here with you next week for more exciting chronicles of the early church, the Holy Spirit, and the continuation of all that Jesus did and taught.

STOP AND READ: Acts 2:14–47

- **Peter started his message by quoting the prophet Joel (Joel 2:28–32).** This excerpt talks about God's promise to pour out His spirit on His people. I love that Peter used Scripture to testify to the Spirit. Peter's choice to highlight God's Word didn't stop the Holy Spirit, but rather fanned the flame of what the Holy Spirit was already doing. The work of the Spirit through this miraculous event led to a deeper understanding of the Word of God. By quoting Joel, Peter was showing that the day marked the beginning of the fulfillment of promises found in Scripture.
- **Peter then turned his attention to the resurrection of Jesus**, referencing two more Old Testament passages, this time from the book of Psalms—Psalm 16:8–11 and Psalm 110:1. Peter showed how those passages spoke of a coming Messiah who would be divine and seated at the right hand of God. He told the people in the crowd that this Messiah was Jesus. Jesus lived a perfect, sinless life and took on the full weight of the world's sins in death only to be raised from the grave and conquer death and darkness once and for all.
- **Peter then invited the crowd to come to Jesus.** In verse 38 he tells them to repent and be baptized in the name of Jesus Christ for the forgiveness of their sins. We learn that three thousand people, many who had come from far-away nations, accepted Jesus and were added to the family of God that day!

GROUP GUIDE

week one

DISCUSS AND REFLECT.

- ★ What part of your Scripture reading this week stood out to you the most and why?
- ★ What did this week's Scripture passage reveal to you about God?

LET'S GET REAL.

- ★ Be honest about what your current relationship with the Holy Spirit is like. What scares or intimidates you? What would it look like for you to slowly start listening to the Spirit's voice in your life? Think simple and small to start.
- ★ Is there anything from your past—like for Peter—or in your life right now that makes you doubt God's desire or ability to use you? How did Peter's story encourage you?
- ★ Is there a part of your life where you've been glorifying yourself lately? How can you give that glory back to Jesus?

PUT IT INTO ACTION.

Have a little dream session!

OK, we know you're all just getting to know each other, so we thought you could start by sharing big or small dreams, desires, or plans you feel like God has for your life. As you read from this week's Scripture, remember that you are God's plan A for the world. Have a conversation about some ways you want to partner with the Holy Spirit to bring heaven to earth. We know this can feel a little intimidating, but what a fun way to get to know one another, encourage one another, and maybe get to witness the firstfruits of a great move of God in a friend's life!

ACTS 3–5

Kenz

week two: day 1

Boastin' in God

Acts 3

OK, are you guys ready to see the transformation of these disciples and everyday believers now that they're filled with the Holy Spirit? As you'll read, these guys aren't messing around!

STOP AND READ: Acts 3:1-10

Acts 3 picks up with the apostles Peter and John headed to the temple together. If you'll remember from the Gospels, Peter and John always had somewhat of a low-key rivalry with each other. I always die laughing at the passage in John 20 where John really wanted it to be known that he was faster than Peter. You can't help but notice some brotherly bitterness all over this scene.

Here's the passage with my commentary in brackets:

> So Peter and the other disciple [John] started for the tomb. Both were running, but the other disciple [John] outran Peter and reached the tomb first. [Proud winner, LOL!] He bent over and looked in at the strips of linen lying there but did not go in. Then Simon Peter came along behind him [slowpoke] and went straight into the tomb. He saw the strips of linen lying there, as well as the cloth that had been wrapped around Jesus' head. The cloth was still lying in its place, separate from the linen. Finally the other disciple, who had reached the tomb first [John. Just had to say it one more time.], also went inside. He saw and believed. (John 20:3–8)

As you can tell, John wanted to make it clear that he was the one who got to the tomb first. (LOL!) But thanks to the Holy Spirit, here they were, headed to midday prayer as kingdom bros. (My, how things have changed!) When they arrived at the temple gate, they came across a man begging who couldn't walk.

It's important to know that in biblical times, begging was recognized as a profession. If you weren't able to work in your family business because of a disability, you were expected to support your family through asking for alms. That's probably why in Acts 3:2 we learn the beggar was carried to the temple gate each day. My personal guess is that a family member dropped him off on their way to work at the family business (maybe carpentry, textile work, or selling goods).

As Peter and John walked by the man, he asked them for money. Verse 4 tells us both apostles stopped and looked intently at the man. I can only imagine how pleasantly surprised the beggar might have been when these two stopped to make direct eye contact with him. Most Jews entering the temple probably avoided his gaze as they scurried on by. He probably hoped he was about to receive a large sum of money that could provide for his family for an entire week.

Little did he know he'd be getting something far greater!

TAKE NOTE: What did Peter say to the man in verse 6?

In the name of Jesus, Peter told the man to walk! He reached out his hand and actually helped lift the beggar to his feet. Luke tells us that "instantly the man's feet and ankles became strong" (3:7). His legs were healed! This was miraculous.

Let's examine three things from this incredible act of healing:

1. **"Silver or gold I do not have" (3:6).** By the world's standards, Peter didn't have much to offer that man. But through the authority given to him by Jesus, he was able to give him something worth far more than silver and gold. By the power of the Holy Spirit and through the faith of two ordinary men, the beggar was transformed into a walking testimony.

We're often tempted to fall into the habit of letting the things we "lack" convince us that God can't use us. I love how Peter admitted what he lacked while boasting about whom he knew.

Dang, we've got to sit with this for a second.

When was the last time you actually "admitted" what you lacked in a moment of insecurity? I don't know about you, but this is so hard for me. So often I put up walls, shrink back, and let my insecurities rob me of the relationship or conversation, when really these moments have the potential to turn into something miraculous.

From this passage of Scripture, it's clear to me that God loves to move through those who aren't as focused on what they *don't* have as they are on what they *do* have. And that's the power of the Holy Spirit. So let's learn from Peter and start boasting about whom we know—Jesus!—rather than hiding behind what we think we lack.

REFLECT ON THIS: Do you think you've been using anything you "lack" as a cop-out in your faith? If so, name it!

Why have you let this hold you back from letting God use you?

2. **"In the name of Jesus Christ of Nazareth" (3:6).** Jesus was a Nazarene, meaning He was from Nazareth. During biblical times, being from Nazareth wasn't exactly cool. Throughout Jesus's ministry, people referred to Him as "Jesus Christ of Nazareth" as an insult. But here we see Peter reclaiming this title and using it with total pride and power. (We love a low-key jab at the system!)

Peter made it very clear where the healing power resided—with Jesus! It was the power of the name of Jesus that counted here. After all, it was the mention of His name that not only healed a chronically disabled man, but gave him the strength to jump and shout praises to God. Peter explained to the crowd gathered there that it wasn't through his own power that the man was healed—it was by faith in Jesus. Peter simply trusted in someone who *did* have the power to make the miraculous happen.

STOP AND READ: Acts 3:11–16

FILL IN THE BLANKS: Acts 3:16

By ________________ in the name of ________________, this man whom you see and know was made strong. It is Jesus' ________________ and the ________________ that comes through him that has completely healed him, as you can all see.

3. **"Then he went with them into the temple courts, walking and jumping, and praising God" (3:8).** Keep in mind that this man spent every day of his life sitting outside of the temple courts, on the fringe of both the temple and society. I love how after his legs were healed, he walked into the temple with Peter and John and worshipped with everything he had! He immediately used the gift he'd received to honor God.

TAKE NOTE: The Scripture says this man was healed because of what (3:16)?

STOP AND READ: Read the rest of Acts 3 to see what happened next (3:17-26).

A crowd gathered in astonishment at the complete healing of this man. Peter wisely took advantage of this group of people gathered together and told them about the saving power of Jesus Christ. Peter knew faith didn't just come from hearing or seeing miracles; it came by knowing the person and power behind the miracle, just as this man did.

This is so important! In Romans 10:17, Paul writes this exact sentiment to the church at Rome: "Consequently, faith comes from hearing the message, and the message is heard through the word about Christ."

Acts of the Spirit are meant to point to Jesus. They aren't magic tricks meant to impress. Miracles are markers of the power of Jesus, softening people's hearts so they're willing to receive His good news. That's why in Acts 3:19–21, Peter offered an invitation to the crowd to repent of their sins and follow Jesus.

As we close out today, get honest with yourself about areas of your life where you've been taking credit or glory rather than giving it to Christ. This is often really hard to admit, so take a good look at each and every area of your life. You aren't alone in this; the temptation is real! But as we see through the first portion of Acts, healing and salvation happen when we bow before the name of Jesus so only He is seen.

I believe that like in the early church, miracles upon miracles will erupt in your life as you allow the Holy Spirit to flow through you without a need to be noticed.

REFLECT ON THIS: When was the last time you intentionally or unintentionally took the credit or spotlighted yourself instead of the Lord?

What was the result of that, and what might you want to say to Jesus in response?

week two: day 2

Be with Jesus

Acts 4

Yesterday we read about Peter and John healing a man at the temple. The people who witnessed this were amazed, so Peter took the opportunity to share the gospel with them. The church is growing, and this is so exciting. But of course there would be some haters! Let's open our Bibles to Acts 4 and see what these grumps have got to say.

STOP AND READ: Acts 4:1-4

TAKE NOTE: Who's included in the group of people that approached Peter and John while they spoke to the crowd (4:1)?

When Acts 4 picks up, we find the religious leaders in Jerusalem very unhappy with Peter and John. The priests, the captain of the temple guard, and the Sadducees (part of the religious elite) apprehended the two apostles during their preaching. Verse 2 tells us two of the reasons they were upset:

1. **Peter and John were preaching.** The religious elite believed the law permitted only priests to instruct the people in spiritual matters, especially in public. (Whoops! Offense *numero uno*!)

2. **They were teaching about the resurrection of Jesus.** The Sadducees didn't believe in resurrection or even the possibility of an afterlife. Part of their worry about Peter and John's message was that Jesus offered a pretty convincing argument for the resurrection "from the dead." (Strike *numero dos*!)

Because of these two offenses, and because these men held power, Peter and John were thrown into jail for the night. Despite this setback, though, Luke gives us some incredible news in verse 4: "But many who heard the message believed; so the number of men who believed grew to about five thousand."

Wow! This deserves an all-out praise party! Despite the obvious opposition from the religious ruling class, the church grew. Remember, at the last count in Acts 2:41, after Pentecost, three thousand people were accounted for. But here the early church has grown to five thousand, not including women and children. Despite the power plays, threats, and intimidation from the leaders of the day, the church was gaining believers. More people were deciding to follow Jesus, not fewer!

STOP AND READ: Keep reading Acts 4, verses 5–22.

The next day, Peter and John were brought before the Sanhedrin, essentially Jerusalem's Supreme Court, to plead their case. In verses 5 and 6 we learn that the list of people who opposed them had quite literally grown overnight, including rulers, elders, scribes, Annas the high priest and his family, Caiaphas, John, and Alexander. Don't forget about the priests, the captain of the temple guard, and the Sadducees from the day before. This crowd asked Peter and John, "By what power or what name did you do this?" (4:7).

Peter, full of the Holy Spirit, responded, "It is by the name of Jesus Christ of Nazareth" (4:10).

Jesus Christ of Nazareth. The man whom the Scriptures prophesied was the coming Savior of the world. The man they crucified. The man who rose from the dead. Peter boldly declared that *Jesus* was the one who healed the beggar at the temple gates.

This stumped the Sanhedrin. Although still resistant, they seemed to comprehend that something about this band of believers and the man they followed was different. Luke's description of their response is one of my favorite passages in all of Scripture. Let's look at verse 13 together: "When they saw the courage of Peter and John and realized that they were unschooled, ordinary men, they were astonished and they took note that these men had been with Jesus."

These men had *been with Jesus*. It really was and still is that simple! There wasn't anything special about Peter or John. They weren't formally trained or extremely gifted. They'd simply spent three years of their lives walking with, learning from, and absorbing everything about Jesus. Their time spent with Him was the difference maker. It gave them a new courage and boldness to stand up to their opposers and a purpose and mission that were unstoppable.

Don't you love that? Just like Peter and John, we have the everyday opportunity and invitation to *be with Jesus*. We can be transformed and emboldened through time with Him. Yet I wonder how many of us have been putting time with Jesus on the back burner. How many of us have spent more time trying to become extraordinary or impressive on our own terms? How many of us have lost sight of the power of being with Jesus?

Even the Sanhedrin couldn't help but admit that these two ordinary men had been with Jesus. And because of it, their lives were made different.

REFLECT ON THIS: Which answer best describes your time with Jesus lately?

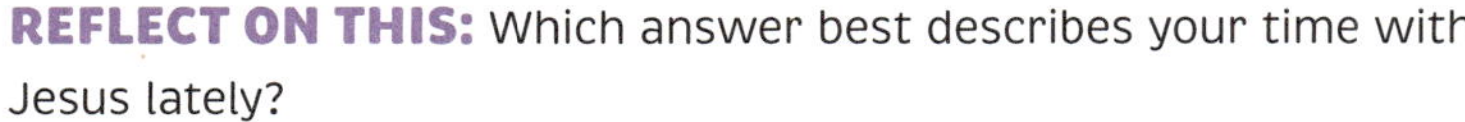

What tends to keep you from being with Jesus?

I'm constantly blown away by the powerful simplicity of being with Jesus. My heart often wanders, but eventually I find my way back. There's truly no place I'd rather be than in His presence! My walk with Jesus, my relationships, and my ministry underwent amazing transformations when I made time with Him my top priority.

Do you need breakthrough? *Be with Jesus.*

Do you want transformation? *Be with Jesus.*

Do you need healing? *Be with Jesus.*

Do you crave influence? *Be with Jesus.*

Do you want to walk in boldness? *Be with Jesus.*

Do you want to be made new? *Be with Jesus.*

Like Peter and John, let's strive to be a generation marked by this simple observation: *They've been with Jesus.*

How cool that by doing this study, you're already actively spending time with Jesus through studying His Word. Yet I wonder what other ways you might be able to be with Jesus this week. Maybe it's through prayer? Maybe it's acknowledging His presence in the little moments? Maybe it's worshipping in your car? Perhaps it's through simply sitting and listening for His voice.

You might not have time at this very moment, and that's OK. But look at your day or week and carve out a few minutes (maybe even a whole hour) to simply be with Jesus in some other creative ways. I know you know this, but I'll just remind you: There's no better way to spend your time. There's no better mentor, there's no better therapist, and there's no better friend than Jesus.

REFLECT ON THIS: How else do you want to spend time with Jesus this week, and when will it be?

week two: day 3

What We Can Learn from the Early Church

Acts 4

Before we finish up our story from Acts 4 we started yesterday, let's take a look back at a few things I think are super important.

STOP AND READ: Flip back to Acts 2 and read verses 42–47.

Don't those verses give you all the warm and fuzzy feelings inside? A part of me wants to camp out in this passage forever. This is what the early church community looked like!

Remember, this group consisted of people from all over the place. What was supposed to have been a two-week pilgrimage for the festival of Pentecost turned into an extended stay. Those who already lived in Jerusalem opened up their homes and broke bread with these new followers of Jesus. I'm sure they had their fair share of problems, but still, this was true Christ-centered community in action. They bore each other's burdens, shared meals together, and fell more and more in love with Jesus every single day.

REFLECT ON THIS: What specifically stands out to you about Acts 2:42–47?

Did you catch the second part of verse 47?—"And the Lord added to their number daily those who were being saved." The church was growing! There was something attractive, compelling, and intriguing about this makeshift community of believers. People were coming to know Jesus and fully committing to the family of God.

REFLECT ON THIS: This is a tough question, but is your love for Jesus attractive? Are people drawn into a relationship with Jesus through the way you live? Reflect on why or why not.

Although a recent study on the state of the church "suggests signs of renewal, particularly among younger generations"—in part because of increased church attendance[1]—most people today are under the impression that the church is dying. Statistics have shown fewer people showing up on Sunday mornings, membership numbers down, and physical church buildings sitting empty. But what changed that led to the church losing its attractiveness? What's different? Certainly not Jesus!

As we finish our story from Acts 4 and think back on all we've studied in Acts so far, take note of markers of the early church that perhaps differ from the church we're familiar with today. I think there's *so* much to learn from these early Christians about how to bear fruit as the body of Christ.

OK, OK. It's time to get back to our biblical *Law & Order* episode! (*dun, dun, dun* . . .) The members of the Sanhedrin were so perplexed by Peter and John that all they did was command them to never teach in the name of Jesus again, threaten them with future punishment, and let them go.

STOP AND READ: Now read back through Acts 4:13-22.

Peter and John immediately returned to their church family and shared the great news! Let's imagine for a second that there was a whole crowd gathered, anxiously waiting for a full report of what had happened. Maybe kids ran around outside as the adults stood huddled together, pacing back and forth in anticipation. I can almost see Peter and John strolling into the room, giving out hugs and high fives as they recounted the details: "We told them about Jesus! All they could say was that we were like Him. They told us not to talk about Him anymore, but we told them no!"

What an amazing scene! Let's finish the rest of the chapter together.

STOP AND READ: Acts 4:23-37

FILL IN THE BLANKS: Acts 4:29

> Now, Lord, consider their threats and enable your servants to
>
> speak your word with ____________ ______________________.

Verse 24 tells us that in response to Peter and John's report, the believers immediately prayed in confident unity. They praised God for who He was (4:24), they prayed in light of His Word and His promises from the Old Testament (4:25–28), and they asked for more boldness, more power, and more signs and wonders (4:29–30).

Their prayers were answered right away as the Holy Spirit filled the room and, like an earthquake, shook every believer's heart and even the walls around them. Every person was filled with the Holy Spirit and proclaimed the Word of God with unrestrained boldness. Wow!

Time for a pause

I want to spend some time reflecting on several things I noticed about the early church, things that encouraged and challenged me about the type of community I want to create and surround myself with. Rather than your seeing this as a legalistic checklist, my hope and prayer is that it inspires you to radically fight for and pursue these characteristics in your own faith communities. Our churches, Bible studies, friend groups, and ministries don't have to feel stale and systematic; they can be vibrant, attractive, and alive—just like the Acts church.

1. **The Acts church was quick to pray.** We've already seen prayer in action several times throughout Acts. In Acts 1:24, the disciples prayed before choosing someone to replace Judas. In Acts 4:24–29, after facing persecution from the Jewish leaders, the community of believers praised God and prayed for boldness to continue spreading the message about Jesus.

Trust me, time and time again throughout Acts, you'll see the early church respond with prayer. Their first response was always to take their cares, worries, needs, and desires to the Lord. I believe the family of God would radically change if we stopped making prayer our backup plan and instead made it our primary posture.

REFLECT ON THIS: Do you pray with your community? If not, what's stopped you?

2. **The Acts church was empowered by the Holy Spirit.** Let's flip back to the book of John and read about the heart-to-heart Jesus had with His disciples in the upper room.

STOP AND READ: John 14:9-14

TAKE NOTE: What does Jesus say will happen when He leaves (14:12)?

Jesus is basically saying they'll get to see even greater miracles and wonders when He leaves because they'll have the power of His Spirit living *inside* of them. And guess what! In Acts 4, we see this coming true, just as it did at Pentecost (Acts 2:4). The disciples were crazy enough to believe that what Jesus had said was actually going to happen. They were empowered by the Holy Spirit to do the miraculous, say the tough stuff, and step out in boldness!

The Acts church was where illnesses were healed, struggling people were redeemed, demons were cast out, and darkness was pushed back. The early followers of Jesus had a unique sensitivity to how the Spirit was moving in, through, and all around them. We've already seen them tap into the supernatural in the first four chapters of Acts, and there's a lot more to come.

So many faith communities today choose to discount or ignore the power of the Holy Spirit, while the people in the early church went out of their way to acknowledge and pursue it. The Spirit was their connection to Jesus and their invitation into His mission.

Let's be empowered by the Spirit!

REFLECT ON THIS: How do you see the Holy Spirit at work in your community—or is His work honestly not noticeable?

Reading this part of Acts, what excites you about bringing the power of the Holy Spirit–dwelling in you, a believer–to your community? What do you desire to see happen?

3. **The Acts church was unified in a divided society.** Acts 4:32 shows us a kind of unity that many of us have never experienced. The early believers were all of one heart and mind, centered on Jesus. They didn't see anything as uniquely theirs but rather generously offered up all they had for the good of the body. In this community, people cared way more about the needs of their brothers and sisters than they did about their own. This kept them united in the midst of persecution, political turmoil, and uncertainty.

Notice that in the beginning of Acts, Luke describes how the body of believers were constantly *together*. They were at each other's homes, they met in the temple courts, they broke bread with one another. This community wasn't just "united" for the sake of a mission statement or optics; they were united in ordinary moments.

I love how God moves when His people come together as one body!

REFLECT ON THIS: What's keeping you from being "one in heart and mind" with your community as described in Acts 4:32?

4. **The Acts church spoke unashamedly about Jesus.** We read about this when Peter and John told the Sanhedrin, "As for us, we cannot help speaking about what we have seen and heard" (Acts 4:20). Then the body of Christ prayed, "Now, Lord, consider their threats and enable your servants to speak your word with great boldness" (4:29).

The early church cared more about God's opinion than peoples' opinions. This led them to proclaim the good news of Jesus in everything they did. Even when it was against the grain of culture or got them in trouble, the name of Jesus was always on their lips. Many Christians today (including me at times) hide their beliefs in certain settings because they fear what others might think about them.

But I want to proclaim my love and trust in Jesus proudly and boldly. I want my life and words to tell this truth: Following Jesus is the best thing that's ever happened to me.

Let's be unashamed in our love for Jesus!

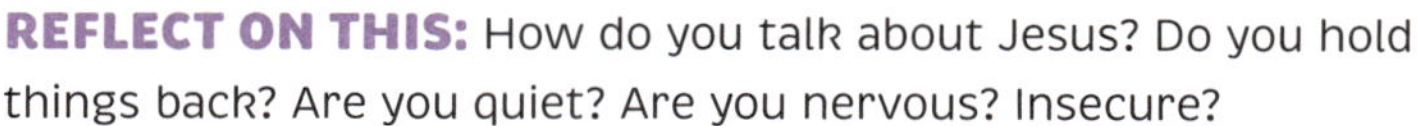

REFLECT ON THIS: How do you talk about Jesus? Do you hold things back? Are you quiet? Are you nervous? Insecure?

What conversations do you have with your friends about your faith?

What's another marker of the early church you've noticed in the first four chapters of Acts not mentioned in my list?

As we close today, I want to ask you this: How are you challenged to make your community more like the early church? Because I'll be the first to admit that my community hasn't looked like this, and it still doesn't look like this—for a couple of reasons.

The obvious reason and my main excuse is that I recently moved across the country, so everyone's new and leaning into community takes time. I say it's an "excuse" jokingly, because the truth of the matter is I could use the whole "I just moved" reason for months longer than I should. Although community takes time to build, we have an opportunity to speed up the process through some of the things we just learned.

But the second and more vulnerable reason is that I just can't seem to put myself behind me. When I hang out with people, I think about *me*, I talk about *me*, I hope they like *me . . . me, me, me*. So when I read about the church here in Acts, this selfish mentality truthfully looks disgusting.

I want to partake in a community that isn't about me but about ministering to those around me. So yeah, it's safe to say I'm challenged to take ownership of where I've missed the mark, and I hope to see my community look a lot more like this.

REFLECT ON THIS: Which marker(s) of the early church do you want to see more of in your faith community?

- Quick to pray
- Empowered by the Holy Spirit
- Unified in a divided society
- Speaking about Jesus unashamedly

How can you take ownership of where you've missed the mark and help your community look more like the early church?

week two: day 4

Why Holiness Matters

Acts 5

After yesterday, did we all just have a heart-to-heart with our community? Or is it just me? I know, I know. It's probably just a day later and you didn't have time for that, but I do hope it happens. Gosh, this book will get ya!

Let's keep reading, but . . . *warning!* This section isn't as mushy and gushy as yesterday's. Two people die. Yeah, you read that right!

STOP AND READ: Acts 5:1–11

How are you feeling? We're only eleven verses into chapter 5, and some major stuff just went down. If I were reading this study for the first time, this is the point when I'd close the book and go watch an episode of *The Bachelor* to lift my spirits. But hang with me here—let's try to piece together this story, ask the right questions, and seek God's heart.

TAKE NOTE: What husband and wife duo is this story about (5:1)?

What did Ananias and Sapphira do with the money from the sale of their property (5:1–2)?

Think back to our Scripture reading from yesterday. Who else sold their property and gave the earnings to the apostles? *(Hint: We didn't talk about him directly. Look toward the very end of Acts 4.)*

If you said Barnabas, then you answered correctly! At the end of Acts 4, we see that it was common practice to sell property and give the earnings to the apostles for ministry. This generous act probably garnered a lot of respect and honor within the community. It wasn't required, but it was celebrated! I'm guessing that Ananias and Sapphira saw how people responded to Barnabas's generosity and coveted the same recognition for themselves.

But here was the problem: Even though they copied the outward act of generosity in the name of Jesus, their intentions were deceitful. Barnabas gave his gift with a sincere and honest heart, but the same couldn't be said for Ananias and Sapphira. Hidden behind their good deed was pride, selfishness, and dishonor. They wanted to *appear* generous without actually practicing generosity.

Oof. This is tough, because I'd be lying if I said this sin hasn't shown up in my own life in different ways.

REFLECT ON THIS: Why do you think Ananias and Sapphira were literally struck dead because of their sin?

I think Luke is reminding us that the early Christian community was the new temple and was to be taken seriously. Remember when we talked about this in Week One? When the Holy Spirit came at Pentecost, God's personal presence took up a permanent residence in the hearts of His people. The body of Christ was the new living and breathing temple.

If you know anything about the temple, you know it was an incredibly holy place. Some Old Testament stories include instances of people being struck dead in the presence of God because they were "unfit" to stand in His holiness. That's why only a high priest was permitted to go into the "holy of holies" once a year after undergoing various kinds of ceremonial cleansing precautions.

Here in Acts, Luke shows us more evidence of how the temple had become flesh through God's people. This story of Ananias and Sapphira reminds us that God meant serious business when He sent the Holy Spirit to dwell inside of us. And this excerpt from N. T. Wright's commentary on Acts 5 sums it up perfectly:

> If we watch with excited fascination as the early church does wonderful healings, stands up to the bullying authorities, makes converts to right and left, and lives a life of astonishing property-sharing, we may have to face the fact that if you want to be a community which seems to be taking the place of the Temple of the living God you mustn't be surprised if the living God takes you seriously, seriously enough to make it clear that there is no such thing as cheap grace.[1]

At this point in Acts, God was quite literally building His church from the ground up. That's why this mattered so much! It was the first act of intentional sin from within the family of God we read about after Jesus ascended. To put it simply, Ananias and Sapphira could not stand in the presence of the holiness that marked the church at this time. That led to a dismal outcome for them—they were struck dead because of their deliberate deception and manipulation of the Holy Spirit within them. Verse 11 tells us how the church responded to this incident.

FILL IN THE BLANKS: Acts 5:11

Great ____________________ seized the whole

____________________ and all who heard about these events.

The reaction was a deep understanding of the weightiness of what it meant to be a follower of Jesus and to truly carry His holiness within.

OK, let's get real and talk about holiness!

In our modern church world, we love grace, we love mercy, and we love abundance, but we don't often love the idea of holiness. It infringes on our comfort and convenience, which we tend to value most. To me, the essence of holiness is perfectly invoked in one of my favorite psalms from King David—Psalm 139: "Search me, God, and know my heart; test me and know my anxious thoughts. See if there is any offensive way in me, and lead me in the way everlasting" (verses 23–24).

Holiness is an every-moment-of-the-day invitation for God to search our hearts and for us to not to be defensive. Holiness means giving God access to the secret compartments of your heart where you hide your bitterness, pride, self-interest, fear, judgment, and other "quiet" sins.

Holiness may hurt, but it's not an optional extra in life with God. It's directly tied to the deepest place of intimacy with the Lord, and it makes us look more and more like Jesus. Holiness isn't a legalistic measuring stick but an instrument of grace that transforms us and chisels away the parts of our hearts that aren't devoted to Jesus.

REFLECT ON THIS: Can you think of a time when your inner heart didn't match your outward expression of faith? Name it here. *(It's OK to admit it. We've all been there!)*

What scares you the most about holiness?

After reading about the seriousness of God sending His temple presence to dwell in you, name one thing you sense needs to be removed or cut out from your heart or spirit.

One of the powerful by-products of taking *holiness* seriously is that the people around you often begin taking *Jesus* seriously. We've seen it throughout history, and you've probably seen it unfold in your own life too.

I often get a glimpse of this in my marriage. Some seasons one of us is just more on track with Jesus than the other, and I can't say it's usually me. Josh is so good about consistently getting in the Word, initiating times of prayer, and striving to live generously. I, on the other hand, can slack sometimes—yeah, your Bible study leader isn't as perfect as you thought she was. (Kidding!)

But I'm so grateful for a spouse who always encourages me to get back to it! He doesn't have to tell me "Read your Bible more"; he just keeps doing it himself. The alarm goes off, he gets up, grabs his Bible, and spends time with Jesus. Eventually I'm influenced to get my lazy butt up out of bed and spend time with Him too!

My point is that holiness in other people doesn't go unnoticed. It's attractive, and it's a brilliant way to have an impact and influence on the community that surrounds you.

REFLECT ON THIS: In what specific ways do you sense God calling you to take holiness more seriously?

STOP AND READ: Finish reading the remainder of Acts 5, verses 12-41, on your own.

Take notes about anything that stands out to you. Pay attention to how the apostles took holiness seriously. Their discipline unleashed the power of the Spirit into every area of their lives and ministries and woke people up to the good news of Jesus. It's pretty amazing to see the power of the Holy Spirit so active in everyone's lives!

GROUP GUIDE

week two

DISCUSS AND REFLECT.

- ★ What part of your Scripture reading this week stood out to you the most and why?
- ★ What did this week's Scripture passage reveal to you about God?

LET'S GET REAL.

- ★ What has your intimacy with Jesus looked like these days? Have you made the time to be with Him? Or has this honestly not been a priority? Share where you are with the group.
- ★ What has held you back from experiencing depth in communities you're a part of? Is it pride? Nerves? Rejection? Comparison? What's standing in the way?
- ★ What main conviction surfaced when reading the passages about holiness? Do you feel God is gently asking you to let something go?

PUT IT INTO ACTION.

Moment of confession!

We think it's safe to say that this week's Scripture reading surfaced a whole lot of conviction. Maybe you've already shared what that thing is for you. But for some of us, there might still be a quiet sin or tiny bit of shame we haven't shared because this just didn't seem like the right time. But we truly believe saying that thing out loud and practicing confession in community is step one to overcoming it and growing a little closer to Jesus.

So what is that thing? What's standing in the way of holiness in your life? Maybe it has to do with community or spending time with Jesus. If you feel comfortable, share. But if you're still not quite ready, that's totally OK too! We encourage you to think about one trusted friend you could share with this week instead. This takes intentionality and courage, but we promise you it's worth it!

ACTS 6–9

Mac

week three: day 1

The Stephen Mindset

Acts 6–7

Hey, fam! I hope you're loving your journey through the book of Acts so far. We warned you it was going to get a little wild, and as you've already experienced, that's been true. I love that life in the Spirit is the most wild and fun adventure! Let's pick back up in Acts 6 and keep studying. The family of God had multiplied, and as it is with anything that grows, there were definitely some hiccups along the way.

STOP AND READ: Acts 6:1-8

TAKE NOTE: What two groups of people were having issues (6:1)?

In Acts 6:1 we learn that some widows weren't being properly taken care of during the daily distribution of food. Let's get some contextual information so we can fully understand what was happening.

First off, what's the difference between Hellenistic Jews and Hebraic Jews? Well, let me tell you! Hebraic Jews felt more of a connection with Jewish culture and likely came from Judea (aka the region where Jesus had been), while Hellenistic Jews were fonder of Greek culture and came from all over the Roman Empire, otherwise known as the Diaspora.

Tensions had heightened between these two groups, so the apostles decided to do something about it. It's not clear that there was deliberate wrongdoing in the distribution of the food; it seems like more of a miscommunication or lack of leadership.

So for the apostles to give their full attention to prayer and the teaching of the Word, they delegated and raised up a new group of people to handle these issues. In essence, the new leaders were administrative assistants who helped ensure fairness in the practical details of serving widows. This was the appointment of the first deacons. The Word says the seven men chosen were of good reputation, full of the Holy Spirit and wisdom (6:3). Sounds like a solid bunch to me!

After the seven were selected, the apostles laid hands on them, prayed over them, and released them to do the work they were appointed to do. We'll talk more about "laying hands" later.

Acts 6:7 says, "The word of God spread. The number of disciples in Jerusalem increased rapidly, and a large number of priests became obedient to the faith." Yes, you read that right—a large number of *priests* proclaimed Jesus! These could have been the very same priests who persecuted Jesus not that long before, now fully awakened to the love of God. Big things were happening all around the early followers of Jesus!

Let's keep moving. But I feel like I need to mention that I have a love/hate relationship with what happens next.

STOP AND READ: Acts 6:8-15

TAKE NOTE: Who was the man who performed great signs and wonders among the people (6:8)?

Time for a pause

Before we really dive in, I want to have a heart-to-heart with the women who sometimes feel like they're second-best or go unnoticed in the kingdom of God. If that's you, gather around and lean in. Verse 8 says, "Now Stephen, a man full of God's grace and power, performed great wonders and signs among the people." And you might be wondering, *Who is this Stephen guy?* Start by looking back a few verses.

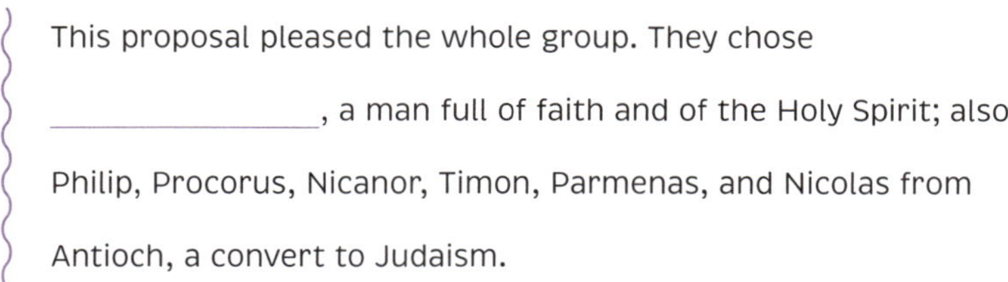
FILL IN THE BLANK: Acts 6:5

This proposal pleased the whole group. They chose ________________, a man full of faith and of the Holy Spirit; also Philip, Procorus, Nicanor, Timon, Parmenas, and Nicolas from Antioch, a convert to Judaism.

Stephen was one of the early church's newly appointed deacons who oversaw service projects like the one that cared for widows. Stephen wasn't the front man of the early church—he wasn't Peter or John, or even one of the lesser known apostles. His leadership role wasn't necessarily about teaching the Word of God to the masses, healing the sick, or representing the community. He had a behind-the-scenes administrative role.

But Acts 6:8 just told us Stephen was far from a quiet or timid little follower of Jesus. Over the course of Acts 6 and on into Acts 7, we see Stephen used in extraordinary ways. He performed signs and wonders, preached incredibly powerful sermons, received a powerful vision, and as the first ever Christian martyr, he was killed because of his unshakable faith in Jesus (we'll get to that in a second).

What I love about Stephen is that he didn't allow his title, his assignment, or his experience to limit him. He didn't leave the work of ministry or deeply knowing the Word of God to the big dogs. He stepped into his appointment to serve the church without seeing it as a closed door or a limitation. Trust me, Stephen wasn't a second-rate apostle or a stand-in for Peter when the latter couldn't make it to the temple on time. *God set apart Stephen for something special too!*

Based on my own journey and experience, my guess is that a lot of you feel as if your appointment in God's kingdom is far less glamorous and exciting than that of some of the other believers you know. Maybe you feel like you'll never measure up, like you're constantly living in someone else's shadow or not cut out to lead. Maybe you're frustrated with the seemingly small opportunities God has placed in your hands.

Let Stephen's story bring you hope and challenge you all at the same time! You are *not* second-best. You are *not* meant to function only as a substitute for others. What God has placed before you is *not* inferior to what He's placed before your friend.

I encourage you to take on a Stephen mindset in this season. You are set apart for something *amazing*! I don't care if your résumé has blank spaces. I don't care if you've been denied every opportunity you've applied for lately. I don't care if you can't pray, speak, write, sing, or lead like that other woman. I believe God wants to use *you*.

God might have you in a season of life when you're not "in charge," but that doesn't mean you're incapable or unimportant. Stop underestimating what God can do in and through you! I want to see more and more women say a complete and humble yes to whatever God wants to do in their lives, even when the process is slow—and especially when it looks different from their friends' stories or the stories of some super well-known Christian speaker/singer/whatever (think of the women you tend to admire most).

REFLECT ON THIS: Does somebody hold an opportunity, appointment, or position you constantly find yourself coveting? Name it here.

What would it look like for you to take on a Stephen mindset? For what has God perhaps set you apart?

As you read through Acts 7 next, pay close attention to the power, grace, and humility Stephen demonstrated. Let your heart be encouraged as you see how he radically surrendered his will and lived for Jesus.

STOP AND READ: Acts 7

REFLECT ON THIS: How do you feel after reading Acts 7? What emotions came up?

After Stephen's passionate, powerful, and (let's be honest) long-winded response to the high priest, in verse 54 we see that his fate did not look good. Stephen said yes to being used by God no matter the cost. Although the outcome was tragic, in his final moments Stephen trusted that he would soon be with the Christ he loved.

TAKE NOTE: What did Stephen see when he looked up to heaven? Include all the details (7:55-56)!

This isn't the only description in Scripture of Jesus being at the right hand of God the Father. This image is depicted throughout Scripture, which means it matters! Let's look at two other examples of this imagery.

FILL IN THE BLANKS:

> Matthew 26:64: "You have said so," Jesus replied. "But I say to all of you: From now on you will see the Son of Man __________ at the ________ ________ of the Mighty One and coming on the clouds of heaven."

> Colossians 3:1: Since, then, you have been raised with Christ, set your hearts on things above, where Christ is, __________ at the ________ ________ of God.

In both these verses, it's very clear that Jesus is seated at the right hand of God. I think it's important to note that when *Stephen* saw a picture of heaven, Jesus was standing. Why is that?

We can't know for sure, but I do know when people stand rather than sit, it typically marks excellence and praise. That's why we stand at the end of incredible musicals or plays or when someone important walks into the room. Our choice to stand often means we believe there's something worth honoring.

I like to believe that in Stephen's vision, Jesus stood as a beautiful act of solidarity. This honored Stephen for the important yet difficult work he was about to complete. Maybe Jesus gave Stephen a standing ovation, communicating to His beloved that he would be welcomed home with open arms.

Maybe that's why Stephen was full of grace, willing to receive his fate. With the picture of Jesus standing before him in his mind, he exhibited the same posture of forgiveness Jesus had on the cross: "While they were stoning him, Stephen prayed, 'Lord Jesus, receive my spirit.' Then he fell on his knees and cried out, 'Lord, do not hold this sin against them.' When he had said this, he fell asleep" (Acts 7:59–60).

The text describes the stoning of Stephen as delicately as possible, but I'm sure it was a heartbreaking sight for any follower of Jesus who witnessed his death that day. But there's an incredible undercurrent here that we can't miss.

TAKE NOTE: At whose feet did the witnesses place their coats (7:58)?

This is a powerful moment. A Jewish Pharisee named Saul of Tarsus supervised the stoning of Stephen. Starting tomorrow, we'll read about Saul leading the charge in the intense persecution of the early followers of Jesus.

Now, this is a bit of a spoiler alert, but Saul would soon be converted into one of the most faithful followers of Jesus the world has ever known. Although the end of Stephen's story is tragic, confusing, and heartbreaking, God in His mysterious ways takes broken pieces and turns them into something beautiful. In this case, Stephen's graduation to heaven intersected with Saul's pathway into the kingdom of God.

I can't wait to be back with you tomorrow to pick up in Acts 8, learning more about Saul and the spread of the gospel by the early church.

week three: day 2

Imparting Versus Impressing

Acts 8

After the heaviness of yesterday, let me just say we're in for a serious treat for the rest of this week's reading! It's much happier than last week and contains some of my absolute favorite stories in Acts. But before we pick up where we left off, I want to remind you where we've been since we started this journey together. So let's review:

The book of Acts is a letter from Luke to his friend Theophilus (unless, as we said, that's a symbolic name he used to write to a wider audience). The letter is about the continuation of all that Jesus did and taught. Remember, this was the second in-depth letter Luke wrote, the book of Luke being the first. Acts 1 tells us that before His ascension, Jesus left the disciples with specific instructions. We've looked at Acts 1:8 before, but today let's look at what He told them with new eyes! See if you can fill in the blanks without looking back.

FILL IN THE BLANKS: Acts 1:8

> You will receive power when the __________ __________ comes on you; and you will be my witnesses in __________, and in all __________ and __________, and to the ends of the earth.

We know from Acts 2 that the Holy Spirit did indeed come. The Spirit fell on the apostles and everyone gathered with them at the time, giving them the unique ability to speak in many different languages. This happened during the festival of Pentecost, when Jews scattered all over the world made a pilgrimage back to Jerusalem for their religious duties and celebrations.

These Jewish visitors encountered the apostles and were stunned when they received the message about Jesus the Messiah and the resurrection in their native languages. The apostles called them to repent, adopt God's upside-down ways, and live under His rule. The result was thousands of Jews deciding to stay in Jerusalem and join the movement.

The early church grew and gained influence in the city of Jerusalem. Needless to say, the Jewish leaders at the time were less than thrilled. In fact, they were so threatened by this new movement that they killed one of its leaders, our beloved friend Stephen.

It feels like we've come to the end of our story. *The church?* Under attack. *The people?* Afraid for their lives. *The message of Jesus?* Considered blasphemy by the religious rulers. These certainly weren't great conditions for the early church to flourish!

Because Jerusalem was no longer safe, many of the early followers of Jesus fled to the surrounding areas called Judea and Samaria. Those names should sound familiar. Remember Acts 1:8? Jesus said this exact thing would happen! The tragic death of Stephen became the catalyst for the spread of the gospel into its next phase: "in all Judea and Samaria" (1:8).

That's where our story picks back up today. For the first time in Acts, we're going to see the good news of Jesus leave the city walls of Jerusalem and penetrate the hearts of some of the most unlikely people. It's such good stuff, so let's jump in!

STOP AND READ: Acts 8:1-24

Acts 8 starts with an update about Saul. We're going to talk a lot more about him later this week, but what you need to take away now is that Saul and other Jewish leaders led a period of intense persecution. Believers were forced to scatter into the countryside, while the apostles stayed put in Jerusalem.

In the Greek language, two different words represent the English word *scattered*. The first word implies scattering in the sense of making something disappear or break apart. The second word implies scattering in the sense of planting or sowing seeds, the kind of scattering that leads to widespread growth. That's the word used in Acts 8:1.

This scattering marked the beginning of something new (8:4–5): "Those who had been scattered preached the word wherever they went. Philip went down to a city in Samaria and proclaimed the Messiah there."

In Acts 8 we meet another one of the deacons who, like Stephen, was chosen in Acts 6 to help coordinate service for widows.

TAKE NOTE: What was that deacon's name (8:5)?

Because of the persecution of the early church, and presumably with guidance from the Holy Spirit, Philip traveled to Samaria in northern Israel. You might remember from Jesus's parable about the man we call the Good Samaritan that Jews and Samaritans considered themselves enemies, harboring deep dislike and even hatred.

Generally speaking, they didn't get along. It's all a bit confusing, but most scholars chalk it up to the intermarriage between pagans and lower-class Jews some six hundred years earlier, when Assyrians conquered the area. Jewish people of that time essentially turned their noses up at the Samaritan people, convinced they were "less than." But boy oh boy, things were about to change!

Philip began to teach about Jesus in Samaria, even performing miracles and wonders like casting out demons and healing the sick. The crowds in Samaria received this good news about Jesus as the Messiah, and the city was filled with an uncontainable joy (8:8). Don't you just love that?

As we keep reading, we learn about a guy named Simon the Sorcerer, locally famous in Samaria as a magician. I believe Luke includes this story about Simon to create a stark contrast we need to pay attention to. Like Philip, Simon was able to do things that seriously amazed people. Luke doesn't tell us exactly what those things were, but the power this guy had definitely wasn't given by Jesus. The works Stephen and Philip did were for the glory of God, but this wasn't the case with Simon. Acts 8:9–12 directly states the difference.

STOP AND READ: Reread Acts 8:9-12 as a refresher.

Simon *impressed* the people while Philip *imparted Jesus* to the people. Simon was all about momentary goose bumps, while Philip was all about encounters that led to lasting change. Simon's acts put himself center stage, while Philip's acts put Jesus center stage. Outwardly, their signs and wonders may have looked the same, but inwardly their hearts and motivations were radically different.

Time for a pause

Let's sit in this tension together for a while.

At first, I'm quick to think, *Oh! I am definitely a Philip and in no way do I relate to Simon,* then read right past this story. But if I sit and let the Holy Spirit perform a thorough investigation of my heart, I realize I'm perhaps more like Simon than I would care to admit. How many times have I posted online hoping somebody scrolling along would see me as beautiful, important, or impressive? How many times have I stood before a group of women teaching the name of Jesus while doing my absolute best to appear wise, in control, and worthy of their attention?

Heck! Even while writing this book, little thoughts have slipped into my mind, questioning how my writing will make me appear to readers. My heart often seeks to *impress* before it ever seeks to *impart.*

REFLECT ON THIS: Confess a time when you sought to be impressive.

Be brutally honest about your personal experience with trying to impress. (Double check yourself if you're about to choose *It's all about Jesus 100 percent!*)

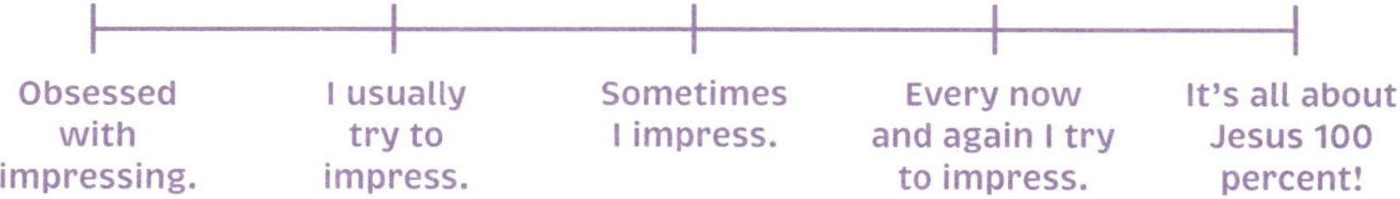

If you're about to do a quick search for the definition of the word *impart,* let me save you the trouble. (After all, I'm giving you the top result from Google, so it's definitely trustworthy information!) *Impartation* in relation to Christianity is defined as "the ability to give unto others that which God has given to us. It is the transference of spiritual 'gifts' from one man or woman of God to another, especially through the laying on of hands."[1]

Do you see the difference between impressing and imparting? Impressing results in temporary impact, while imparting leaves an eternal impact. Impressing is all about the *gift*. Imparting is all about the *giver*. That's the difference between Philip and Simon, and I think it's what Luke tried to convey. When we simply impress people with our skills, gifts, talents, or abilities, people see only *us*. But when we impart the gifts God has given us without seeking recognition, people see *God*. Impartation transfers Jesus to people's hearts. That's eternal!

I don't know about you, but I don't want to be a woman known by her own platform; I want to be a woman who passionately shows off the platform of Jesus. I want to be a woman quick to impart before she ever aims to impress. I want to be like Philip, who through Spirit-given gifts invited a whole Samaritan town into a relationship with Jesus.

REFLECT ON THIS: Think about the definition of impartation: *to give unto others that which God has given to us*. How can you posture your heart and life to impart rather than impress?

What's one specific way you can begin practicing impartation today?

week three: day 3

A Different Kind of Fire

Acts 8

Today we're picking our story back up in Acts 8. Samaritans, including Simon, accepted Jesus and were baptized. When the apostles back in Jerusalem received news of this, they sent two men to lay hands on the new believers and pray for the baptism of the Holy Spirit in their lives.

STOP AND REREAD: Acts 8:14–25

TAKE NOTE: Who did the apostles send to Samaria (8:14)?

Remember back in Week One, when I said reading Acts in light of the book of Luke was of the utmost importance for a complete understanding of this text? I'm about to put those words into action! Let's go back to Luke for some history on why this moment matters so much.

STOP AND READ: Flip back to Luke 9 and read verses 51–56.

TAKE NOTE: Where are the disciples in this story (9:52)?

What do they ask in verse 54?

In this story the disciples were with Jesus as they all traveled through Samaria back to Jerusalem. Somewhere along the way they faced opposition at a Samaritan village that refused to welcome Jesus. (Remember, there was a lot of hostility between Jews and Samaritans.) The disciples were offended by this, so James and John (who were brothers, the sons of Zebedee) asked Jesus a peculiar question.

FILL IN THE BLANKS: Luke 9:54-55

> When the disciples James and John saw this, they asked, "Lord, do you want us to call ____________________ down from heaven to ____________________ them?" But Jesus turned and ____________________ them.

This question makes me laugh! Did they really think Jesus would say "Sure, guys! Go ahead and call down fire from heaven. Set this village aflame, and then let's head on to Jerusalem!" Like . . . no! Absolutely not!

Of course, Jesus rebuked them, and they kept moving. This story might feel a bit random in the book of Luke, but remember this is a two-part volume. So let's flip back over to Acts to pick up the story and make sense of this moment.

Peter and John (the same guy who asked if he could set a town on fire) were sent to Samaria to pray for the arrival of the Holy Spirit. Just like in the book of Luke, again we find ourselves in the context of Samaritan villages. I believe these two stories, both written by Luke, are meant to be seen side by side. When we compare them, we see that the very same apostle who wanted to call down fire in judgment traveled to Samaria to call down a different kind of fire—*the Holy Spirit!*

FILL IN THE BLANKS: Acts 8:15-17

> When they arrived, they prayed for the new believers there that
> they might receive the ______________ __________________,
> because the Holy Spirit had not yet come on any of them;
> they had simply been baptized in the name of the Lord Jesus.
> Then Peter and John placed their hands on them, and they
> __________________ the Holy Spirit.

This gives me goose bumps! It's a beautiful picture of the redemptive purposes of God as John grasped the true mission of Jesus. In Luke 9 he thought something like *Look at these unworthy people. Let's judge them now.* But armed instead with the mission of Jesus and the knowledge of the resurrection firmly planted in his heart, John returned so he could lay hands on the very same people and ask for baptism of the Holy Spirit. Verse 17 tells us that's exactly what happened when they asked—the Samaritans received the Holy Spirit.

Reading this story of God's redemptive power at work in John makes me wonder about my own heart and life and the people or places on which I'm quick to call down the fire of judgment. I wonder if perhaps Jesus is leading me to call down a different kind of fire. Maybe instead of incessantly arguing with the same people over and over again, we can choose to at least figuratively lay hands on them and pray for the Holy Spirit to come. I believe they need a different kind of fire—not flames of destruction, but flames of the Spirit that daily transform us!

REFLECT ON THIS: Have you been low-key calling the fire of judgment down on somebody in your life? If so, confess it here!

What would it look like to call a different kind of fire down on them—the Holy Spirit? How could you begin practicing that in your life?

OK, things are about to get super cool!

STOP AND READ: Acts 8:26-40

TAKE NOTE: Who are the two main characters in this story?

Who told Philip where he was to go and what he was to do (8:29)?

This is an incredible story of how a probably very wealthy Ethiopian eunuch came to proclaim the name of Jesus. I hope you paid attention to how Philip imparted Jesus to the man rather than simply impressing him with knowledge. Also notice how this story highlights the inclusivity of the gospel. God sent Philip to quite literally chase down this man from Ethiopia, even though the early church hadn't yet traveled to Africa. This story reminds us that the gospel is for *everyone* and that God will stop at nothing to chase down all His kids.

I love that God was the one who sent Philip directly to this man through an angel of the Lord, and then the Spirit told him where to be and what to do. Once Philip entered into conversation with the Ethiopian, he simply told him who Jesus was and what He'd done on our behalf. Verse 35 tells us he told him the "good news about Jesus."

Something in Philip's story and presentation compelled the Ethiopian man to want to get baptized immediately. He stopped the chariot, stepped down, and practically ran to the waters. How beautiful!

I wonder who the Spirit might be leading each of us to tell about the good news of Jesus. Perhaps more than ever before, pay special attention to the Spirit's voice in your life this week. Who is He highlighting for you? What special promptings are being placed on your heart? Where are you feeling compelled to go?

I don't think this is something that happened only for Philip in Acts. I believe God is still speaking, calling us to go and tell the good news of Jesus to the world around us. What's so beautiful is that He will be the one to send us and lead us every step of the way. *It's that simple!* Who might the Spirit be sending you to?

REFLECT ON THIS: Ask God these few questions and then listen for what the Spirit might want to say in return. Jot down anything you hear, even if it feels weird or you don't understand.

- God, who specifically do you want me to share the good news of Jesus with?
- What do you want me to know about them?
- What would it look like specifically for me to go to them and tell them about Jesus?

Finally, don't breeze over the last two verses (39–40), when Philip low-key traveled through space and time. It's just cool, and I don't want you to miss it!

week three: day 4

Eyes Wide Open

Acts 9

We made it to Acts 9! And we're about to witness a famous conversion as Saul, the ruthless persecutor of Christians, becomes the bold preacher of the good news of Jesus.

It's an exciting story and carries a *ton* of meaning. Without the conversion of Saul, we wouldn't have thirteen of the twenty-seven books in the New Testament. Not to mention, who knows how long it would have been before the gentiles (*gentile* means non-Jewish) heard the gospel! In a lot of ways, Saul's conversion is the hinge on which the church we know today swings.

Now, remember, when we last read about Saul, he was into persecuting Christians *big time*. Where we pick up in Acts 9, not much has changed. It's important to note that Saul was a Pharisee by vocation. Pharisees were scholars of the law; their role in society didn't include serving as judges or police. Despite the fact that his career didn't involve violence, Saul zealously picked up a glorified side hustle: hunting down and arresting followers of Jesus, then dragging them to Jerusalem to undergo a trial. This became his passion project, and horribly, his *mission*. Saul inspired literal terror in the early followers of Jesus.

What's most encouraging about this story is that Saul serves as a prime example that there's hope for literally *anyone* to encounter Jesus! If the love of God could reach Saul, an intentional murderer of Christians, then we can have faith that nobody is too far gone. *Nobody!*

On the flip side, what's perhaps most disturbing about this story is that Saul truly believed he was doing the work of God by killing Christians. It's a bit scary to think that somebody could be so sure about something and yet ultimately so wrong. We have to remember that we are human beings trying to comprehend the infinite vastness of our good God's heart through tiny slivers of understanding. Saul's story of repentance reminds me we're called to be people of strong conviction who simultaneously hold our beliefs with humility. We won't always get it right! But we have the Holy Spirit within us to chisel and refine us.

Saul had it so very wrong. But after a powerful encounter with Jesus (and a big ole helping of humble pie), God used him in some of the most extraordinary ways the world has ever seen.

I hope you're as excited as I am to finally see Saul become a good guy!

STOP AND READ: Acts 9:1–22

TAKE NOTE: Where was Saul headed (9:2)?

What happened to him as he neared his destination (9:3)?

Saul went to the high priest and requested permission to head to Damascus to begin persecuting Christians there. (I guess the Jerusalem scene was getting a tad too mundane for him.) Damascus was a city about 130 miles northeast of Jerusalem, and it would have been a six-day journey altogether. The community of believers in Damascus must have been fairly prominent for Saul to travel all that way. This indicates the church was indeed growing rapidly all throughout Judea.

The high priest gave his permission, so Saul and some of his buddies left for Damascus. But just before they arrived in the city, something wild happened: "Suddenly a light from heaven flashed around him. He fell to the ground and heard a voice say to him, 'Saul, Saul, why do you persecute me?'" (9:3–4).

A light shone down from the heavens and knocked Saul to the ground. My guess is that Saul was high-key *shook*. A voice from heaven asked, "Saul, Saul, why do you persecute me?"

My mind immediately wants to know one thing: Why did Jesus say Saul's name twice? Since Luke had only so many words to share this story, I'm guessing there's some significance in Jesus repeating Saul's name. Let's stop for a second and, to give us some context, look at other times Jesus repeated a name. Flip back to each of the verses below and fill in the repeated name.

FILL IN THE BLANKS: Luke 10:41

"______________________, ______________________"

FILL IN THE BLANKS: Luke 22:31

"______________________, ______________________"

FILL IN THE BLANKS: Luke 13:34

"______________________, ______________________"

When Jesus repeated a name, it seems like He was trying to get undivided attention from the person He was about to speak to because what He was about to say was of great significance. It's kind of like when you're in trouble and your mom uses your full name. Even in my early thirties, whenever I hear my mom say "MacKenzie Leigh Bridges" I know to zip it and listen up.

That leads me to believe the question Jesus asked Saul mattered greatly: "Saul, Saul, why do you persecute me?" Take note that even though technically it's the early church being persecuted—not Jesus himself—Jesus still asked this question of Saul.

You see, Saul had been going after Jesus's bride (the church), and Jesus wasn't having it! Jesus took it as a personal attack. *I love this!* Jesus is so joined to His people that you cannot touch them without touching Him.

Think about this: Your incredible union with Jesus means that whatever happens to you, He feels himself. You are so united with Jesus that He would describe something happening to you as something happening to Him—personally.

When you're in the middle of a storm, He endures that storm with you.

When you're brokenhearted, He feels that heartbreak with you.

When you're full of joy, He experiences that joy with you.

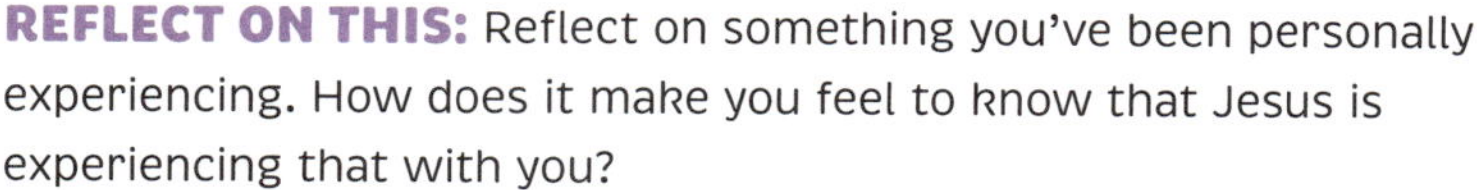
REFLECT ON THIS: Reflect on something you've been personally experiencing. How does it make you feel to know that Jesus is experiencing that with you?

Acts 9:5–6 tells us Jesus revealed His identity to Saul and told him to go into the city (Damascus) to await further instructions. The men who traveled with Saul had no idea what had happened. In fact, they hadn't seen anything at all. Verses 8 and 9 bring a plot twist: "Saul got up from the ground, but when he opened his eyes he could see nothing. So they led him by the hand into Damascus. For three days he was blind, and did not eat or drink anything."

Saul's eyes were open, but he couldn't see a thing! This new physical blindness matched the spiritual blindness he'd been walking in—his eyes wide open to the law but unable to give grace and mercy.

He spent three days in Damascus without his vision, so disturbed by the whole experience that he didn't eat or drink at all. I can imagine him there, sitting in silence, hungry and confused. I'm sure he internally wrestled with all that he'd known and done before.

In verse 10, a disciple named Ananias enters the story. The Lord called to Ananias in a vision and told him to go lay hands on a man named Saul staying in Damascus, to restore Saul's sight. Ananias hesitated at first, because the rumor around town was that Saul was the very man who had come to Damascus to persecute followers of Jesus. And honestly, I don't blame Ananias in the slightest! If Saul had come to my town, I would have run for the hills. But God told Ananias He had a special calling set aside for Saul, and that Ananias needed to go at once.

Ananias entered the home where Saul was staying, laid hands on him, and spoke these words: "Brother Saul, the Lord—Jesus, who appeared to you on the road as you were coming here—has sent me so that you may see again and be filled with the Holy Spirit" (9:17).

OK, how much do you love that Ananias called him "Brother Saul"? That warms my heart! We can't forget that Saul was blind, so it would have been comforting for him to hear a voice of warmth and love. Just three days before, Saul and Ananias were enemies. But through Jesus, they became brothers. I love the family of God!

FILL IN THE BLANKS: Acts 9:18

Immediately, something like ____________________ fell from

Saul's eyes, and he could ____________________ again. He got up

and was ____________________.

After the prayers of Ananias, scales fell from Saul's eyes and he regained his vision. He could see the physical world again and gained spiritual sight for the first time. Perhaps that's why the first thing he chose to do (before even eating or drinking) was to declare his newfound faith through baptism.

Check out verse 20 to have your mind blown! Your Bible might say "at once," "immediately," or "within the hour" Saul was in the synagogues in Damascus preaching about Jesus and proclaiming that He was the Son of God. Talk about an extreme makeover! Saul was truly a new man in Jesus Christ.

REFLECT ON THIS: Think back on your own Jesus transformation moment or on your season of life, then reflect on how, like Saul, you're now able to "see" differently.

What can you see now that you weren't able to see before?

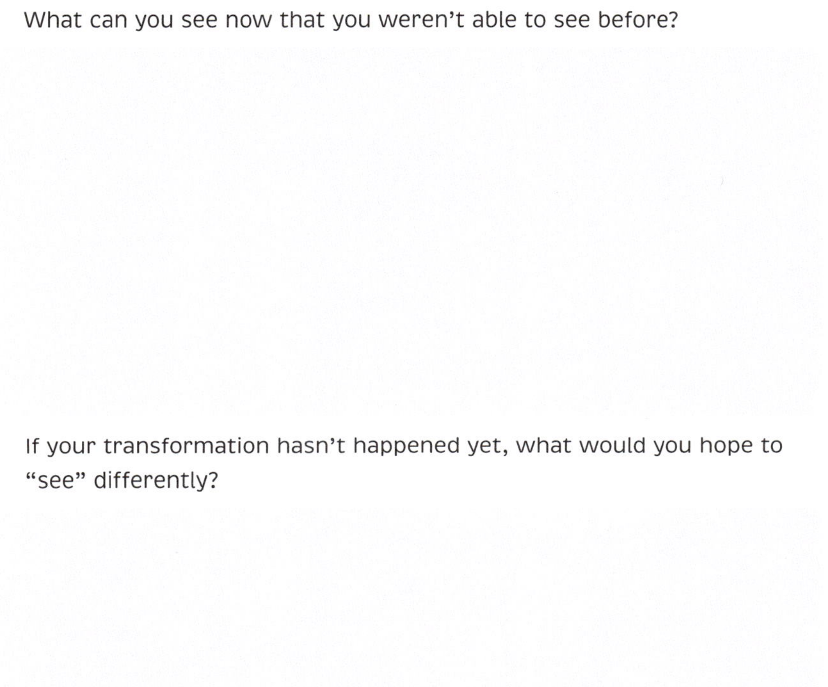

If your transformation hasn't happened yet, what would you hope to "see" differently?

Now, things would definitely not be all rainbows and butterflies for Saul from this point forward. Remember, in Acts 9:16 God told Ananias, "I will show him how much he must suffer for my name." The road Saul was about to embark on would be gloriously full of Jesus but also full of hardship and suffering. As you finish reading Acts 9 on your own, you'll see some of these difficulties start to unfold. Saul had to escape Damascus because of plots to kill him, he faced rejection in Jerusalem, and then he was sent back to his hometown of Tarsus because there were even more death threats against him. Acts 9 also has some super cool stories about a healing and a woman being raised from the dead.

STOP AND READ: Acts 9:23–43 *(Jot down any notes or things of interest to you as you read.)*

Next week we'll be back with Acts 10 and the story of the first gentile presented with the good news of Jesus. Love you, fam! I'm already counting down the moments until we're back together.

GROUP GUIDE

week three

DISCUSS AND REFLECT

- ★ What part of your Scripture reading this week stood out to you the most and why?
- ★ What did this week's Scripture passage reveal to you about God?

LET'S GET REAL

- ★ After reading Stephen's story, can you recognize any limitations you've put on your life or ministry that you want to break off in the name of Jesus? What are those limitations?
- ★ We talked a lot about judgment and humility this week. How are you hoping to grow in humility? Be specific.
- ★ Were you convicted when reading about impressing versus imparting? In what moments are you most tempted to try to impress? What would it look like for you to impart instead?

PUT IT INTO ACTION

Testimony time!

We don't know how well you all know each other, but we thought it would be great to have a little testimony moment in your group and share the story of when you came to know Jesus for yourself. When did you know you wanted to give your whole life to Him? What was the transformation you saw in your personality or character? Take some time to share with your group and get to know where you all are in your faith journey. How fun!

ACTS 10–13

Kenz

week four: day 1

The Family Gets a Lot Bigger

Acts 10

Welcome back to another week in Acts! This week our story takes place in a beach town called Caesarea on the shores of the Mediterranean Sea. This town might sound familiar because it's easily mistaken for Caesarea Philippi, mentioned in the Gospels as the place where Peter proclaimed Jesus as the Messiah. But the Caesarea we're talking about this week was a Roman city about seventy miles from Jerusalem where the Roman governor of the province of Judea lived.

As we study Acts 10, picture a coastal town where the bright blue sea meets the beige of a sandy beach, with intricate stone structures almost camouflaged in the sand. Can you see it? I love knowing this beautiful scene is where we'll see the gentiles officially welcomed into the family of God.

STOP AND READ: Acts 10:1-48

In verse 1, Luke introduces us to Cornelius—a Roman centurion and a devout man who feared God. You might be asking two things:

What's a centurion? Well, a centurion was an officer in the Roman army. Cornelius was in charge of around a hundred other soldiers stationed in Caesarea.

He feared God? I thought he was a Roman! Luke tells us Cornelius was a man of devout faith. He had more than likely been exposed to the concepts of Judaism and was supportive of the faith, but he wasn't circumcised and hadn't adopted the full lifestyle of Judaism. This meant it was ceremonially unclean and taboo for a Jew to enter Cornelius's home.

In verses 3–5 we learn an angel of God had appeared to Cornelius and told him to send his servants to Joppa, where a man named Simon Peter was staying. Cornelius obeyed God's command and sent two servants and one soldier to collect Peter from Joppa, about thirty miles away. The next day, while the men were still journeying to the city, Peter went to the roof of the house where he was staying to pray.

While in prayer, Peter enters a trance-like state where he has a vision of a great sheet descending from the sky. On the sheet are all kinds of unclean animals God commands Peter to eat! Peter tries to refuse because, since childhood, he'd been trained in the law to avoid unclean animals. But in verse 15, God says to Peter, ""Do not call anything impure that God has made clean."

TAKE NOTE: How many times was this vision repeated?

It's important to note that the number three marks new life and transformation all throughout the Bible—including Jesus being in the tomb for three days! Well, the number three also holds great significance in the life of Peter. He denied Jesus three times and was redeemed in a similar fashion on the shores of the Sea of Galilee. I don't think it's an accident that Luke tells us that the events in Peter's vision happened three times. This moment was significant for Peter. We're about to see a huge transformation unfold with new life being offered to the gentiles through Peter preaching the good news of Jesus. I love it!

As Peter tried to process the vision from God, the Spirit told him what was about to happen—three men were looking for him, and he had to go with them. Then the men Cornelius sent arrived and asked to see Peter, explaining that they were sent by Cornelius after a "holy angel" appeared to him. I wonder if Peter felt overwhelmed as reality echoed what the Spirit had said. This truly *was* the work of God!

Peter invited the travelers to come in and stay the evening as his guests. Because the men were gentiles, this offer went against every custom of the Jewish people. I truly think Peter was beginning to uncover the significance of his dream on the roof. I can picture him staying up all night in full anticipation and conversation with God, wondering what was about to unfold.

The next day Peter, the three men sent by Cornelius, and a few other believers from Joppa began their journey to Caesarea.

FILL IN THE BLANKS: Acts 10:24

> The following day [Peter] arrived in ____________________.
>
> Cornelius was ____________________ them and had called together his relatives and close friends.

Don't you love that Cornelius was waiting with anticipation for them to arrive? He had such hope and trust in God that he invited his friends and family over to be a part of the welcoming party. Don't forget, Cornelius did what the angel of God asked of him, but he had no idea what the result would be—or whether Peter even existed!

I wish I had faith like Cornelius had. Sometimes I sense God speaking in my life, but I look for every disclaimer or backup plan I can find because I'm afraid I might have heard Him wrong, I'll look stupid, or I'll be disappointed. Can you relate? I mean, when was the last time you "full sent"—I mean, truly *went the whole way*—with something God spoke to you like Cornelius did? I can't say I ever have.

REFLECT ON THIS: Did you ever begin to doubt something you were once so confident that God had spoken to you? If so, name it.

Why did you begin to doubt?

Cornelius, however, was so confident in the voice of God that he was willing to look ridiculous in front of his entire community. What if Peter didn't show up? What if he hadn't really heard from God at all? But God in all His goodness didn't disappoint! Peter arrived, and the two men exchanged stories about how God had spoken to them in the days prior.

Peter then preached a brief yet powerful sermon to a large group of people at Cornelius's home, proclaiming the person and power of Jesus to them. We've already read about several of Peter's sermons in Acts. They're usually quite a bit longer than this one, but I suppose it didn't take much for the gentiles to believe in Christ! My guess is that as Peter spoke, Cornelius and his friends had hearts burning for Jesus. Before Peter even finished his sermon, the Holy Spirit fell on them, and they began speaking in tongues.

This is *monumental*. Even with all the Holy Spirit's movement in Acts, it wasn't common for people to receive spiritual gifts immediately after professing faith in Christ. This moment is meant to be a parallel to the Jewish Pentecost in Acts 2. It showed that the gentiles weren't second-rate believers or unworthy of Jesus. The Holy Spirit fell on them the exact same way He had on the first followers of Jesus at Pentecost, and even bigger than that, He fell on the gentiles the same way He'd fallen on the *apostles* at Pentecost. This moment had the seal of approval from the Holy Spirit.

Verse 45 says the Jewish Christians there were stunned and amazed by this act of the Spirit in the lives of the gentiles. This changed everything for them! Peter called for everyone there to also be baptized with water in the name of Jesus. This meant the gentiles were officially part of the family of God!

TAKE NOTE: What details did God have to align for this moment to happen? *(Skim back through the Scripture reading for today.)*

I think this goes without saying, but all this didn't happen because overzealous apostles accidentally stumbled into gentile territory and began preaching like wildfire. God did a lot, and a lot of people had to listen to make this happen. It was meticulous, careful, and intentional.

We could say the same thing about the Ethiopian eunuch's conversion back in Acts 8 and the conversion of Saul in Acts 9. These *intentional* acts of God opened the doors to the family of God even wider. Men and women, gentiles and Jews, and all ethnicities, ages, abilities, and vocations—they would *all* receive the invitation to open up their hearts to Jesus and be made new.

REFLECT ON THIS: How does this truth from Scripture change your everyday life?

How do you feel compelled to respond to the intentional things God has placed in your life?

Over the last few years, people have often asked me, "What's one thing you would say to your younger self?" My answer is always the same. I would tell myself it *all* mattered! The coffee dates, the prayers, the late-night conversations, the setups, the teardowns, the time and preparation . . . it all mattered.

As we mentioned in the introduction to this study, while in college Mac and I started what's now a national ministry. That ministry led us to do what we're doing now (writing Bible studies for you all!), but what it is now is not what it was a decade ago. It was basically a simple yes to start a small group, then a leap of faith to invite a bunch of people, then a few more yeses and a lot more faith paired with a whole bunch of action. More than a dozen years later we can see that all of it mattered.

Not that our story is anywhere near as cool as the one we just read in Scripture, but I can confidently say the Lord does miracles through our simple acts of obedience.

I don't know where you are in your life right now, but I know for certain that God wants to use you in an unbelievable way if you'll let Him. He wants to speak to you and give you visions of where to go and what to do. He wants to stand beside you as you make bold decisions for the kingdom of God. He wants to endure the journey with you, start the thing, make the move, and all the while be right by your side. My prayer is that Cornelius and Peter inspired you to tune in a little closer to God's voice and see just what He might do through your simple yes!

REFLECT ON THIS: How can you position yourself, your time, and your life to hear God's voice more clearly?

What might be standing in the way of that for you?

week four: day 2

Judgment Versus Teamwork

Acts 11

To jog your memory, we just finished reading Acts 10, where we learned about our gentile turned passionate follower of Jesus, Cornelius, and our guy Peter, who had the opportunity to share the good news of Jesus with a bunch of gentiles. The church was growing day by day through ordinary people just like you and me.

Now we'll jump back into Scripture and see what happens next. Peter had traveled back to Jerusalem, but by the time he arrived, word had already spread, and some people weren't so happy with some of the decisions he made.

STOP AND READ: Acts 11:1–18

TAKE NOTE: Who criticized Peter (11:2)?

REFLECT ON THIS: What is your impression of the group of people from this passage?

First off, "circumcised believers"? What a dreadful identifier—even if circumcision *was* super important to this group! Why did Luke decide that was a good idea? I personally would not like to be part of a group with that designation.

Second, I hope I don't have to define the word *circumcision* for you. If you need help, though, and decide to search the internet, look for "circumcision *in the Bible*" just to be safe. Adding the word *Bible* makes any potentially risky internet search safer (LOL). I can't be held responsible for your search results if you forget that!

OK, so back to the circumcision believers. To put it bluntly, these were the grumpy, super religious, annoying people of the early church. They had strong opinions and weren't afraid to let everyone know about them. Acts 11:2 tells us they "criticized" Peter.

Peter retold the story from his own perspective and pointed out that God placed His seal of approval on the baptism of the gentiles (11:4–17). He even reflected on what Jesus had said before His death about baptism: "Then I remembered what the Lord had said: 'John baptized with water, but you will be baptized with the Holy Spirit.' So if God gave them the same gift he gave us who believed in the Lord Jesus Christ, who was I to think that I could stand in God's way?" (Acts 11:16–17).

Luke tells us that after Peter's testimony of the events, these circumcision believers had no further objections; they even began to *praise* God for what He did in Caesarea! But trust me, this is not the last we'll hear from them. They have plenty more complaining to do throughout the book of Acts and the rest of the New Testament.

Time for a pause

I want to use this story to discuss how I believe we should read Scripture. For some of you this is second nature, but for others this might be new. You've probably noticed how we've already begun to use the technique I'm about to explain during the last few weeks of our study.

Whenever I come across a passage of Scripture, the first thing I try to do is understand it within its biblical and historical context. I ask so many questions of the text! I want to know the meaning behind words I don't understand, where the story is happening geographically, what was culturally relevant at the time, and how it fits into the larger story the Bible is telling.

This is why actually *studying* Scripture is so important. It's more than reading a story—it's a lifelong pursuit of understanding to recognize and apply the nuances and meanings we often miss during our initial analysis.

The Word of God is *so much more* than just a historical or literary document. It's a recorded version of the voice of God speaking to us every single day.

Then once I've sought to understand a passage in its original context, I use it as a mirror: I hold it up to my own life and see how it can convict, challenge, and change me.

For example, let's look at this story about the circumcision believers' criticism of Peter. We've spent the last few weeks researching the context of this story, and now we know so much more about why the salvation of the gentiles offended them. But if we're being honest, we have to admit that many of us read that passage and immediately thought this group was a bit ridiculous. We thought, *I would* never *do something like that! I don't care about circumcision, I'm not that petty, and I know what truly matters.*

If we stick to not really understanding this story's original context, we can brush right past our thoughts without any conviction. But remember, we're using Scripture like a mirror, so we have to put this same story into *our* context. We're not harping on and on about circumcision.

But why would we? We're not first-century Jewish men living under Roman control in Jerusalem. We're twenty-first-century women living in the age of social media platforms like TikTok, an ongoing mental health crisis, ordering anything we want from Amazon.com, mega-polarized politics, reality TV, and food delivery like DoorDash.

Our context is different! Or is it closer than we thought?

We might not care about circumcision, but I can guarantee that you and I have some methods or religious systems we've set up to keep others out. We disapprove of people who haven't gone through our particular process to get to Jesus.

If we're judging the Christians next to us with our own set of standards meant to measure their value or worth in the kingdom of God, that's a problem! There's no 10-step program to get to Jesus. We don't get to pick and choose kingdom hierarchy. We don't get to decide our way is better. *There's no right way to get to Jesus!*

You see, this convicts my spirit so deeply. I've got a lot of work to do in my heart when it comes to religious superiority.

REFLECT ON THIS: On a scale of 1 to 10, 10 being the max (Yikes!), how much do you relate to the circumcision believers now?

What personal religious method or pathway have you been glorifying as the best or only way to get to Jesus?

How is Jesus convicting your heart in this area now? What needs to change?

We could've totally missed this important conviction if we had just patted ourselves on the back for not being like the circumcision believers. But by understanding the context behind their struggles, we can understand their situation in the context of our own hearts and lives. When we allow Scripture to speak directly to whatever we hold near and dear, I promise it will reveal more of our beliefs and grow us toward holiness and the likeness of Jesus. I encourage you to use this method as you continue studying and letting God's Word transform you.

In the next portion of Acts 11, we see quite the opposite attitude. We see followers of Jesus actually working together to bring the kingdom of God to their communities, and I just love seeing this teamwork in action.

STOP AND READ: Acts 11:19-26

TAKE NOTE: Who did Barnabas go to find in order to help the ministry continue in Antioch (11:25)?

The first thing you might want to know is that Antioch was considered the third greatest city in the Roman Empire and was known for its business and commerce. But it was also known for its deep immorality. Some might say that, because of this, it was primed and ready for the gospel. The people were desperate for Jesus!

FILL IN THE BLANKS: Acts 11:21

> The Lord's hand was with them, and a ________ ____________
>
> of people believed and turned to the Lord.

Once again, a ton of people turned their lives over to the Lord. Things are just getting better and better!

After leading there for a while, Barnabas left to find Saul, hoping to bring him back so he could assist in teaching the believers in Antioch. My guess is that through the work of the Holy Spirit, Barnabas saw the God-given gifts in Saul and knew this was the place for him to put those gifts to good use. Teamwork makes the dream work, right?

Scripture says that for a whole year, Saul and Barnabas did ministry together in Antioch, and the church thrived. Acts 11:26 tells us the believers there were called "Christians" for the first time. This nickname likely began with undertones of mockery, but ultimately people were associating these men and women with Christ—essentially calling them "Jesus people" or "the party of Christ." (Sure beats the "circumcision believers" group, though!) The believers in Antioch appreciated the name so much that it stuck, and of course we still hear it today.

What we'll continue to see is that Antioch was actually where Saul would take a step forward into the spotlight and into the appointment God had placed on his life to be a messenger to the gentiles. This was his first big debut, thanks to his buddy Barnabas.

All right, let's wrap up this day!

STOP AND READ: Acts 11:27–30

A prophet from Jerusalem named Agabus received a prophetic word from the Spirit about a future famine. The church in Antioch took up a collection for the people of Judea and sent the donations through Saul and Barnabas back to the leaders in Jerusalem for distribution. This was an amazing act of giving as the newly named Christians provided for one another. The message of Jesus was clearly alive in the church at Antioch.

OK, that was a lot, but I hope you received many good insights and revelations from the Word today. We read about the circumcision believers group, who were a little hesitant about Peter welcoming gentiles—but can't we all be that way sometimes? The good news is they changed their minds and got hyped up about the new people added to the kingdom of God.

Then we took a hard pivot and read about the dream team, Barnabas and Saul, absolutely crushing it in Antioch. Some of the Jerusalem prophets even stepped in to help through their tithes and offerings. I'm so encouraged by the body of Christ right now. Hopefully they can keep it up—*eek!*

REFLECT ON THIS: What was your biggest takeaway from today's reading?

What do you feel like your role is in continuing to grow the kingdom of God on earth right now?

week four: day 3

Prayer and Petition

Acts 12

As you guys know, up until Acts 12 the early church had been on a major streak of success, experiencing one exciting conversion after another. But as Jesus promised before He left the earth, things wouldn't always be this exciting (see John 16:33). The enemy was beginning to raise his head with some ugly opposition.

STOP AND READ: Acts 12:1–5

We've reached another tense moment in the life of the early church. In a political move, King Herod (not Herod from the Christmas story, but his grandson) called for the execution of one of the twelve original disciples of Jesus—James. Ugh. Let's just take a moment of silence for James.

It's so easy to read through events like this in Scripture and forget how truly devastating they were. This was the first time one of Jesus's twelve disciples was killed, and James, in particular, was one of Jesus's closest friends. He was one of only three disciples present during the raising of Jarius's daughter (Luke 8:40–56), during the transfiguration of Jesus (Matthew 17:1–13), and as Jesus prayed in the garden of Gethsemane before His arrest and crucifixion (Matthew 26:36–46).

Luke tells us the death of James pleased the Jews deeply, so in an effort to increase his approval rating even more, Herod threw Peter in prison with a plan to put him on trial after the festival of Passover—like when Jesus was tried.

Now, remember that back in Acts 5, Peter escaped from prison. Knowing this, Herod assigned four soldiers to guard him—one on either side of him and two guarding the door of his cell at all times.

FILL IN THE BLANKS: Acts 12:5

> So Peter was kept in ________________________, but the church
>
> was earnestly ________________________ to God for him.

In verse 5 we see that the church began to pray earnestly. The Greek verb used here is *ektenōs*, which means to "stretch out one's hand," the same word used in Luke 22:44 to describe Jesus's prayer in the garden of Gethsemane. These were powerful prayers aligned with the Father's heart. The church members who prayed were deeply dependent on God and felt the need for His intervention in the very depths of their souls.

I wonder if many of our prayers today lack power because they lack true earnestness. Oftentimes we pray for the change we want to see in our lives or the world around us—but half-heartedly. What would it look like for us to pray earnestly, asking God to move?

REFLECT ON THIS: When was the last time you earnestly prayed? What was your prayer about?

What do you want to earnestly pray for right now? How can you stretch yourself out before God as you pray?

STOP AND READ: Acts 12:6–19

While the church prayed, God moved. He sent an angel to wake Peter in the middle of the night and lead him out of the prison unscathed. At first, Peter understandably thought he was dreaming, but then he realized his freedom was the work of the Spirit. He went to the home of Mary (the "mother of John, also called Mark" [12:12]), where many were gathered praying, and knocked on the door.

I love what happens next!

Rhoda, a young girl at the prayer meeting that night, was the one who heard the knocking at the door and went to answer it. When she heard Peter's voice, she was so excited that instead of opening the door and letting him in, she ran to tell the others. They thought she was crazy and told her it was probably his angel (aka ghost?)!

Peter, still stuck outside (LOL), kept knocking until the people finally went to see for themselves. To their surprise it was in fact Peter the apostle, alive and well.

Something about this story is so strangely comforting and refreshingly real to me. It's so . . . *ordinary*! Right in the middle of a huge heaven-sent miracle, a girl made a little mistake and forgot to let in the man she was so ecstatic to see! We all have stories like this, treasured memories we share at holidays year after year. They ring of truth—ordinary, human, believable truth—that makes up our shared human experience.

It would be so easy for skeptics to claim that the story of Peter's miraculous release from prison was just folklore. But if it was just a legend passed down through oral tradition, why would someone include this little snippet of information about Rhoda's human mistake? I say Luke did it so we'd realize everything happened exactly as he described, details and all. Rhoda forgot to open the door for Peter, so nobody believed he was there. But God moved and caused the truth to be known.

REFLECT ON THIS: What might have *seemed* like an insignificant little story or moment in your life that actually pointed to the validity of Jesus and His goodness? Reflect on the warmth realizing this brings to your heart!

Acts 12 concludes with justice for Herod. God wasn't about to let this guy get away with his ugly schemes for much longer.

STOP AND READ: Finish reading the remainder of Acts 12, verses 20–25.

Basically, Herod was trying to be all high-and-mighty, sitting on a throne in his royal robes publicly addressing the people. As you read this passage, you might have observed that some people were convinced Herod must be a god, not just a man. Witnessing this, God decided it was time to intervene and set things straight. An angel struck Herod down, and he was eaten by none other than a swarm of worms. *Yikes!*

I realize this is a crazy moment that can be difficult to understand, but I think Acts 12 displays something beautiful about how God responds to His family. As Christians, we aren't released from the evil in the world. Satan will try to come at us, especially when we're doing awesome things for the kingdom of God. But God is so much bigger and more powerful than Satan. When we respond to crisis or fear by gathering in community for prayer, locking eyes with Jesus, and crying out for help, there's no doubt He'll pull us through.

Scripture doesn't give us a clear timeline from when Herod put Peter in jail to when he was struck down by God. Maybe these two events happened just weeks apart, or maybe Herod still reigned for years before he was killed. But all the while God was looking out for His people. He was watching and waiting for the right time and place, listening to their prayers, and had a plan and purpose in it all.

As we close out for today, I hope you're encouraged to know that God hears your prayers and answers them. As you walk in obedience to Him, there's no doubt He'll pull you through, too, just as He did for the early church.

week four: day 4

Stepping into Your Calling

Acts 13

We're back for another amazing story in the book of Acts. Today we'll start following Saul and Barnabas as they travel from place to place sharing the good news of Jesus, face opposition, and witness God move in miraculous ways. It's an exciting week!

You know the drill. Grab everything you need to do this: your Bible, pens, highlighters, sticky notes, journal, coffee or tea, and probably a snack. (I highly recommend Smartfood Flamin' Hot White Cheddar Popcorn if you need to switch things up.)

Then let's open up to Acts 13.

STOP AND READ: Acts 13:1–3

The last couple of days we were introduced to the church at Antioch, where Saul and Barnabas were commissioned as apostolic evangelists and sent out to teach the Word throughout the Roman Empire. Second only to the church in Jerusalem, the Antioch church would become the most influential body of believers during the early church era. This was due to its large size, multicultural congregation, and anointing with gifts and graces among the leadership and believers.

Verse 1 describes the church and some of its gifted leaders.

FILL IN THE BLANKS: Acts 13:1

> Now in the church at Antioch there were prophets and
>
> teachers: ____________________, ____________________ called
>
> Niger, ____________________ of Cyrene, ____________________
>
> (who had been brought up with Herod the tetrarch) and
>
> ____________________.

So let's get to know our cast of characters! First up is Barnabas, a Jewish Levite from Cypress whom we already know. Then there's Simeon, called "Niger." Niger was a common Roman name, but here the term likely references Simeon's dark skin and complexion. Scholars guess that Simeon was from northern Africa. Next we have Lucius from Cyrene in North Africa. Then Manaen, who Luke tells us was a childhood friend of King Herod the tetrarch, which signifies that Manaen came from a culture of money and high influence.

The last on the list is our pal Saul of Tarsus, a converted Jewish Pharisee who also held Roman citizenship (but more on that later). As we can see already, the church in Antioch ran the gamut of diversity in ethnicities, socioeconomic statuses, and family backgrounds. I imagine this added to the beautiful, dynamic liveliness found in the followers of Jesus in Antioch.

King Herod the tetrarch was the one who beheaded John the Baptist and presided over one of Jesus's trials (Luke 23:7–12). King Herod and Manaen apparently took *very* different paths in life to end up in such opposite roles.

In verses 2 and 3, Luke tells us that as the church worshipped, prayed, and fasted, the Holy Spirit spoke and called for Barnabas and Saul to be sent out to do the work God had planned for them. Members of the church laid hands on these two men and commissioned them with a seal of approval from the Holy Spirit as missionaries of the gospel.

Time for a pause

I want to use this simple moment in Scripture to talk about God-given callings. This is truly one of my favorite things to discuss in context of the Word of God. The story of Saul's life speaks so much to us about calling and purpose because it stands in stark contrast to what many of us believe about our own calling.

Here are a few things we can learn from the life of Saul about finding our purpose:

1. **Stepping into your calling isn't instantaneous.** Although scholars' calculations vary slightly, many believe Saul's conversion on the road to Damascus happened somewhere between AD 33 and 36 and that his first missionary journey (which we're about to look at) occurred between AD 47 and 48. That's at least ten years between his anointing in Acts 9:15 and the official appointment to take the good news to the gentiles. I wouldn't call ten years "overnight"! There was hardship, persecution, and, I'm sure, disappointment aplenty. Saul faced so much rejection that he even had to move back home to Tarsus for a season. Although he saw the miraculous happen around him all the time, that didn't mean he got to miraculously skip the process.

Some of you are frustrated with the pace of fulfilling your purpose because you've set your own timeline, tactics, and markers of success. Hear me say this: True kingdom pace looks *soooo* different from our twenty-first-century hustle pace. You have to trust that God is doing something right here and right now, even if that process is slow by your standards.

Maybe your pursuit of "purpose" has been a glorified hot mess. *That's great!* Maybe you feel behind on the timeline compared to the people around you. *Awesome!* Maybe you're thinking God must not have something in mind for your life because you've been at a standstill for so long. *Stop thinking that!*

If we can learn anything from Saul's life, it's to keep leaning in, keep falling more in love with Jesus every day, and keep trusting that God will use us for a purpose beyond our wildest dreams. Instant callings are like instant coffee—quick to make but a cheap replacement for the real thing. The best cups of coffee come from roasters who know what they're doing, use thoughtfully chosen beans, and take their precious time with the process.

God has hand-selected you, and your purpose is in process with Him. Praise God that we don't step into our callings overnight; it makes the journey so much more rewarding.

REFLECT ON THIS: If you've been anxious to "move on" to the next season of life, where does this anxiety stem from? Or are you content where God has you now? Explain.

How might God be preparing you or using you in a way that perhaps you've overlooked?

2. **Your calling will require you to make sacrifices and leave things behind.** This is going to hurt a little! You ready? *Deep breath . . .*

Your true calling will probably never be attached to comfort and ease. In fact, I'd argue that if you feel all cozy, warm, and safe inside right now, you're not walking in the full potential of God's purpose for you. *Ouch!*

Think about Saul. The choice to step into his calling would be the furthest thing from easy. He was preparing to spend a good majority of his life on the road, away from home, possibly imprisoned, constantly moving from town to town, and never knowing what was ahead. He had no solid ground to stand on other than the message of Jesus. He likely left behind friends, family, possessions, security, and who knows what else.

My guess is that your true kingdom calling will have its fair share of struggles and sacrifices too. You'll be forced outside of your comfort zone, you'll feel like it's unnatural, and you probably won't have a ton of backup plans, shortcuts, or snack breaks. The pursuit of this calling will chip away at the false narratives, lies, undercover sins, and apathy that perhaps you've grown accustomed to carrying. You will definitely have to leave some "stuff" behind if you want to step fully into the ways of God.

In my own life, I've found that my calling to ministry never seems to get easier. I always thought once I had more experience under my belt or more time, it would start to feel like less responsibility or weightiness. But the longer I do it, the more I'm humbled and reminded of my deep need for God to provide and continuously shape me into His image. Every day I feel like I'm surrendering something new and more painful to Jesus than the day before.

You see, your calling will require a lot of sacrifice. But I think my guy Saul and I can both attest to the fact that it's 100 percent worth it to walk right in the center of what God has uniquely crafted you to do. Even in the midst of all the fears, doubts, and challenges, a supernatural peace comes when you move forward in the name of Jesus.

Trust those feelings of peace when things feel daunting, scary, or uncomfortable. Your calling might be just one leap of faith away!

REFLECT ON THIS: Are you afraid to let go of something in your life, instead placing it in front of God's calling for you? What is that thing?

Where do you currently find yourself on the spectrum below?

1–in my comfy zone	5–somewhere in the middle	10–*fully* ready to sacrifice and surrender

3. **Clarity in calling comes when you practice spiritual disciplines.** This may seem simple, but think about what the church leaders in Antioch were doing when they heard about their mission from the Holy Spirit. They were praying and fasting! They weren't doing whatever the equivalent would be to our incessantly scrolling on our phones, or answering every email and text without delay, or spending hours perfecting our sourdough bread recipe. They were in the presence of God asking for answers, ready to listen.

Now, of course there's nothing wrong with checking social media, or answering email and texts, or having a hobby as long as none of that pushes spiritual disciplines into the margins of your life. But maybe God hasn't spoken clarity over your calling because you haven't really been asking Him for answers and then—this is the super important next step—*listening*.

This story in Acts shows us we have a better chance of receiving answers about our calling and purpose when we pray, worship, ask God to speak, and then actually take the time to listen for what He has to say.

There's no infallible method or magical formula to guarantee answers about what to major in at college, what job to apply for next, when to have kids, and so much more women face as life goes on. But there's always an invitation to meet with Jesus. You might not get the answer you wanted, but I believe when we consistently and routinely meet with the Lord, we begin to recognize what His voice sounds like. The voice of God is both gentle and firm—He speaks through the quiet with a whisper, and He also roars over the never-ending noise all around us.

I can guarantee that God is speaking to you, but will you take the time to listen? Will you train your ear to hear what He wants to say?

REFLECT ON THIS: Which of these three points about calling is hardest for you?

What do you sense God is speaking to you regarding your kingdom calling? *(There's no right or wrong way to answer this question! Just write what you feel!)*

I recognize that this is all so much easier said than done, but I hope you're encouraged by the Scriptures and the radical ways God was moving in the lives of the early apostles and in the early church. I know we covered only three verses today, but Mac will pick back up with you next week for the remainder of Acts 13.

GROUP GUIDE

week four

DISCUSS AND REFLECT.

- What part of your Scripture reading this week stood out to you the most and why?
- What did this week's Scripture passage reveal to you about God?

LET'S GET REAL.

- What insecurities or confusion do you have around your kingdom calling? How were you empowered by the Scripture reading this week to take action in the pursuit of God's great plans for your life?
- Cornelius had faith that God would do what He said He would do. What's one thing you're confident that God is speaking over your life right now? What doubts do you have?
- Are you quick to place judgment on people or other believers? Why? Where do you think that judgment comes from?

PUT IT INTO ACTION.

Prayer moment!

We learned a lot about prayer this week and what it looks like to earnestly pray for our brothers and sisters in Christ. Most of us have probably prayed in a group setting before, but we encourage you to step into this a little bit deeper. Rather than passively agreeing, nodding, and moving on to the next person, try to deeply connect with the Father's heart. Try asking for bold things, stepping out in faith, engaging with the Holy Spirit, and actively praying as a group. Share one by one and then pray for one another.

ACTS 13–19

Mac

week five: day 1

The Power of Testimony

Acts 13–14

We're back! And we have a *lot* of Scripture to cover this week. We'll move pretty quickly, but we'll definitely cover the high points of what matters here as Saul (whom we finally know as Paul in Acts 13:9) officially begins his missionary journeys. Remember, after we read about the Holy Spirit setting Barnabas and Saul apart in Antioch for a special mission last week, we talked about calling.

STOP AND READ: Acts 13:4–12

TAKE NOTE: Where in Salamis did Saul and Barnabas proclaim the word of God (13:5), and who went with them as their helper (13:5)?

So Saul and Barnabas set off for their epic journey! This story always reminds me of my first few years after college, when Kenz and I were first starting Delight Ministries, working in ministry together. We traveled the country, visited college campuses, and talked with women about Jesus. We liked to pretend we were girl versions of Saul and Barnabas, on a radical mission for Jesus. Still to this day, we fight about who's Saul and who's Barnabas.

(Honestly, Saul seems a bit grumpier than Barnabas, so I think I win Saul by default. LOL! Sorry, Kenz.)

The missionary power duo made an early stop in a city named Paphos, where they'd been invited to come and share the Word of God by an important, intelligent Roman official.

Sergius Paulus was the Roman proconsul, and Bar-Jesus was a sorcerer and the attendant to the proconsul. The name Bar-Jesus means "son of Jesus," but it seems Luke couldn't stand to call him by that name. So he used the nickname Elymas instead. According to Luke, that name meant "sorcerer" or "magician."

Elymas tried to block the message that Saul (now called Paul) and Barnabas planned to share with the proconsul until *Paul*, full of the Holy Spirit, rebuked him. Verse 11 tells us Paul said Elymas would be struck with blindness for a time, and the declaration came to pass as mist and darkness fell over his sight.

Does this ring a bell? It should! The experience is very similar to Paul's conversion, when he had to go through a time of physical darkness to spiritually see the light. We don't know what happened to Elymas after this, but we do know God was at work.

FILL IN THE BLANKS: Acts 13:12

When the proconsul saw what had happened, he

____________________, for he was amazed at the

____________________ about the Lord.

Paul had just performed a miracle, and yet it was the teaching about the good news of Jesus that ultimately made Sergius Paulus believe in Christ. Signs and wonders are meant to point back to Jesus. Paul's testimony to the proconsul was the tipping point that day.

Time for a pause

Before we keep moving, we have to talk about Saul's new name—Paul! Saul was his Jewish name, and Paul was his Roman name. The choice to go by his Roman name from this point forward probably gave him more credibility with the gentiles. I've always thought the meaning of names is so interesting, so catch this: The name Saul means "sought after," and the name Paul means "little."

To me, this change represents the journey Paul took, leaving behind greatness and significance within Jewish culture in order to die to self and decrease his self-importance for Jesus. All followers of Jesus are meant to do the same! It reminds me of these powerful words from Jesus in Matthew 10:39: "Whoever finds their life will lose it, and whoever loses their life for my sake will find it."

Saul went from an important Jewish leader with a ton of influence, power, and wealth to Paul, a probably very poor and certainly humble missionary who had to rely on the Spirit to be his guide each day. Yet I'm sure his life had never felt more meaningful and joy-filled!

By the way, you have no idea how many times I typed "Paul" while writing this book and had to delete it and switch to "Saul." Praise the Lord that we can finally just call him Paul. Let's just say it together—*Paul, Paul, Paul!*

STOP AND READ: Acts 13:13–52 *(Sorry. This is a long one!)*

Paul and Barnabas left Paphos and sailed to Pisidian Antioch in Turkey (this is different from the Antioch we're familiar with, where the early church had grown). They started out in the synagogue where the local leader invited them to share a message. It was customary to invite visiting guests or teachers to share encouragement or a revelation from their hearts, so Paul shared about the good news of Jesus.

You'll note that in his teaching he included many of the high points, or key moments, of Israelite history that ultimately pointed to the resurrected Jesus of Nazareth being the long-awaited Messiah. This was done intentionally for a Jewish crowd—Paul would have used a different method for gentiles.

Verse 42 tells us the people received the message well and even asked Paul and Barnabas to stay and teach again the following Sabbath. They accepted this invitation, and on the next Sabbath, almost everyone in the city gathered to hear God's Word.

The size of the crowd made the local Jewish leaders seethe with jealousy, and they turned the preaching into a debate. And because some Jewish people rejected the message about Jesus, Paul and Barnabas moved on to preach to the gentiles, who were "glad and honored the word of the Lord" (13:48). The outcome was that "the word of the Lord spread through the whole region . . . and the disciples were filled with joy and with the Holy Spirit" (13:49, 52).

Despite opposition and the two men's eventual expulsion from the city, the message of Jesus had spread—and left a beautifully destructive wake of joy behind. This was good news indeed!

In Acts 14, we'll see a similar pattern alongside some super cool miracles and wonders.

STOP AND READ: Acts 14:1-28

TAKE NOTE: In your own words, what happened in Iconium? In Lystra? In Derbe?

To where do Paul and Barnabas return in verse 26?

FILL IN THE BLANKS: Acts 14:27-28

> On arriving [in Antioch], they ____________________ the church together and ____________________ all that God had ____________________ through them and how he had opened a door of faith to the Gentiles. And they stayed there a long time with the disciples.

I love this! Luke tells us that when Paul and Barnabas returned to Antioch, they gathered the entire church together and shared stories from their travels. I can't even imagine how beautiful this moment must've been. There's such power in sharing testimonies about the goodness of God and the transforming power of relationship with His Son with other believers.

Back in those early days of starting Delight Ministries I mentioned before, we would host a leadership conference in Nashville, Tennessee, where women from all over the country gathered for a few days of training, worship, planning, and fun. We always left a huge chunk of time for what happened in Antioch to happen in Nashville.

After breaking bread together (well, more like tacos), leaders gathered in groups of eight to ten at round tables and simply shared stories of God's faithfulness and work in and through them. They started as strangers, but after two or three hours of sharing testimonies, they felt like family. There's nothing quite like the power of Jesus to bring us all together!

During this time, I always sat back, observed, and basked in the glow of love, hope, and connectedness exuding from every face in the room. Each year I saw tears mingled with laughter, joy bound up with sorrow, and a unifying declaration that Jesus was the one we were all choosing to trust with it all.

If you haven't gathered in a room like that lately, I encourage you to do so. Share your testimonies of God's work and listen with eager ears to the stories of others. Soak in the warmth of being right in the center of a Holy Spirit fire. It will propel you forward and give you a renewed sense of hope.

REFLECT ON THIS: Think about your testimony or stories of God's goodness in your life recently. How do you sense Him moving?

With whom do you feel compelled to share this, and how will you do that?

week five: day 2

Kingdom Conflict

Acts 15

Acts 15 kicks off with more circumcision drama (LOL)! Paul and Barnabas were sent to Jerusalem to speak with the apostles and elders concerning the dispute in Antioch about whether circumcision was necessary to be saved. Go ahead and read it for yourself!

STOP AND READ: Acts 15:1-11

TAKE NOTE: Who stood and addressed the apostles and elders (15:7)?

FILL IN THE BLANKS: Acts 15:11

> "No! We believe it is through the ____________________ of our Lord ____________________ that we are ____________________, just as they are."

It low-key warms my heart to hear from Peter again. I've truly missed him! Peter reminded the council gathered there that the grace of Jesus is what does the powerful work of salvation. It's not any ritual or practice we can do for ourselves—it's all about what Jesus chose to do on our behalf!

STOP AND READ: Acts 15:12–35

Paul and Silas then shared stories about their travels and all they'd seen God do in and through the gentiles. It was almost as if they were saying "*God* has accepted the gentiles; should not we as well?"

Then James (Fun fact: This James is Jesus's half brother) supported what Peter, Paul, and Barnabas had all shared by referencing Scripture from the Old Testament—the book of Amos, which prophesied that this very thing would happen. He then suggested they "should not make it difficult for the Gentiles who are turning to God" (15:19).

They decide to write a letter encouraging the gentiles to abstain from three things.

TAKE NOTE: What were the three things gentiles had to abstain from (15:20)?

Essentially they didn't want the gentile believers acting in a way that would offend the Jewish community and hurt the church's witness among Jews. Abstaining from these three practices helped to ensure that! The council also decided to send two members of its own community (probably Jewish Christians themselves) with Paul and Barnabas back to Antioch, the place where the whole dispute arose, to deliver the message written in verses 24–29. In verse 31 we read that this message was received well by the church in Antioch.

STOP AND READ: Acts 15:36-41

TAKE NOTE: What happens in this passage?

Acts 15 closes with an intense argument between Paul and Barnabas over whether they should take their assistant John Mark with them to check up on the towns they'd already visited. The quick synopsis is that Paul didn't want to take John Mark because he'd abandoned them on their last trip. Barnabas refused to leave him behind, possibly because they were cousins (Colossians 4:10). If we're honest, we can see how this makes sense for Barnabas. Isn't it true that things always get a bit dicey when family is involved?

Take special note of how Luke wrote about this argument. He gave no hint about his opinion of who was right and who was wrong; he just included the story as it happened. So we don't know all the messy details, but part of me appreciates this story. Paul was looking at the situation practically, thinking he needed trustworthy companions. Barnabas was looking at the situation relationally, thinking everyone deserves a second chance. In a sense they were both right, but their determination to *prove* their rightness stood in the way of their calling.

I don't believe Luke included this story to condone getting into arguments with our friends. I believe he included it as an illustration of God's grace. Despite the two men's argument, which could and should have been resolved, *God's mission remained the same*. In fact, Paul and Barnabas's split over this catalyzed two missionary journeys instead of one. God moved despite their human error! That gives me hope and reminds me of my own story.

So many times in my own ministry, I've *so* strongly believed I was right that I ended up in intense arguments with the people I hold most dear. I'm not proud of it, as I'm sure that after a lot of reflection, Paul and Barnabas weren't proud of their own falling out. But when I think back to those moments, I see the hand of God, because those challenges brought some of the deepest levels of grace I've ever experienced.

One of my toughest seasons of ministry and life was when Kenz and I couldn't get on the same page about an important decision. It was incredibly difficult, heartbreaking, and miserable. We both felt deeply hurt and could not understand each other's outlook or motivation. After an embarrassingly long time, we put aside our pride and desire to be right and started picking up the pieces of our broken relationship. It took a lot of prayer, hard conversations, and accountability from other people, but as our relationship healed, I saw God's grace in full force.

Despite my flaws, missteps, and human errors, God still chose to use us together in mighty ways. I'm not sure I'll ever understand why, but the story of Paul and Barnabas choosing to part ways reminds me that fighting for kingdom relationships is so important. God still moved in the midst of their separation, and I've seen firsthand what He can do when we choose to unite despite our differences.

I hope that encourages you in your own friendships and ministry. Like Paul and Barnabas, I know from experience how difficult it is to have conflict within a partnership. If you're facing some relational tension right now, take comfort in knowing you're not alone. But also take action and strive for grace, healing, forgiveness, and purpose in your relationship again.

REFLECT ON THIS: As you read the last few paragraphs, what relationship popped into your mind and heart?

What's keeping you from pursuing healing with that person?

What would it look like to lean into grace and take a step toward reconciliation?

I know it can be difficult to fight for reconciliation, but from my own experience, it's one of the most tangible ways to invite God's grace and power into your life. Today I'm *soooo* thankful God drew Kenz and me back together. It's crazy to think that you wouldn't even have this study if that hadn't happened!

I wonder what hangs in the balance for you when it comes to any relational tension you might be experiencing. Either way, I love that we can trust that in all things God can work it together for our good and the good of those around us.

I'm on your team and in your corner, and I love each one of you! I'll see you tomorrow for another missionary journey with Paul and some hype worship in a jail cell. It's going to be fun!

week five: day 3

Worship While You Wait

Acts 16

Before we dive in today, I want to talk about one little thing. If you're at a point where you've stopped bringing your Bible and you're simply skipping over the **STOP AND READ** sections in this study because you're rushed for time, I encourage you to get that Bible back out!

I'm sure you're all *way* more spiritual than I am, but I have to admit something: When I've done a Bible study in the past, sometimes I've skipped reading the actual Word! I know, I know. You're all judging me right now. I'm judging myself too! But let me remind you of something I needed to hear in those moments:

The words of any Bible teacher, including me, will always pale in comparison to the power of the Spirit-breathed, living Word of God. This book is meant as a supplement to, not a replacement for, reading Scripture and letting the Holy Spirit speak directly to you. Get that Bible out today and dive in with excitement and expectancy!

OK, OK, let's get into it!

STOP AND READ: Acts 16

TAKE NOTE: Who does Paul invite to join him on his journeys (16:1–3)?

Remember that at the end of Acts 15, Paul and Barnabas ended their partnership due to a disagreement over John Mark. Barnabas chose John Mark as his new partner, and Paul chose a man named Silas.

In the beginning of Acts 16, Paul and Silas set off for what we now know as Syria and modern-day Turkey. When they arrived at a city named Lystra, Paul decided to add another member to their team—a young believer named Timothy. Timothy had a Jewish mother and a Greek father, meaning he wasn't circumcised at birth. Because of this, Paul decided to have Timothy circumcised.

But . . . *why?* Didn't Paul say circumcision wasn't necessary to become a full member of God's people? Isn't this one of the reasons he got kicked out of so many towns? *Yes!* But think back to Paul's method for his missionary journeys. He always went to the Jewish synagogues first. It would be much easier for their message to advance if Timothy was seen as a "proper" Jew. So the poor guy was circumcised, and the three men traveled on, preaching the good news and encouraging some of the churches established during Paul's first journey.

Then through a supernatural message given to Paul in a vision, Paul, Silas, and Timothy learned they needed to go to Macedonia. This was exciting new territory for the gospel! Eventually the three men—*and Luke*—arrived in Philippi, the capital city of Macedonia.

Yes, Luke was hanging with Paul! I told you this was coming all the way back in our first week together. Did you catch the narrator's switch from "they" in Acts 16:8 to "we" in Acts 16:10? Luke quietly, humbly joined the story of Acts. He will just as quietly and swiftly disappear in a few verses, but it was great while it lasted!

Again, Paul typically started each visit by teaching in the Jewish synagogue, but in Philippi he left the city and went to a riverbank where a group of women prayed every Sabbath. This fact implies there probably wasn't a synagogue in Philippi, meaning there weren't many Jewish men there. But there were plenty of Jewish women! (Shout-out to the women!) At this makeshift, informal gathering, Paul began to share Jesus with an influential businesswoman, Lydia.

Lydia was a dealer of purple cloth, a luxury at the time, meaning she was quite wealthy. Verse 14 says, "The Lord opened her heart to respond to Paul's message." Although I'm sure Paul's message was powerful and persuasive, God created the real transformation here. I believe this premise remains true today: It's not about gifted teachers, good sermons, powerful podcasts, or crazy conferences; it's about God moving in the hearts of people. That's where true belief begins!

After Lydia and her household were baptized, she graciously opened her home to Paul, Silas, Timothy, and Luke.

In verses 16–22, we read Paul began to irritate a few of the locals when he cast a demon out of a young girl being used to make money as a fortune teller. Angry over the loss of income, her owners took up a case before the Roman leaders in Philippi, causing a huge stir in the city. The Roman officials beat Paul and Silas and threw them in prison to await trial.

I want to camp out in this part of the story for the rest of our time today. Picture this moment: Paul and Silas were in a dark, uncomfortable cell. They were chained, heavily bruised, and beaten. It's not difficult to imagine some dried blood staining their clothes and skin and inescapable cold causing them to shiver as other prisoners stared them down, wondering how their offenses compared.

Things couldn't get much worse.

But then in the midst of the darkness, a song of praise rose from the lips of Paul and Silas. I don't know what they sang that night, although I'm pretty positive it wasn't the most recent worship music smash hit a lot of us have on our playlists. I'm guessing it was their personal favorite song of praise, maybe a rendition of a psalm their mother used to sing, or an old, passed-down hymn from long ago. Whatever it was, it was powerful enough for Luke to note that their fellow prisoners *listened*. Nobody complained or told them to hush. Scripture simply says the other prisoners "were listening to them" (16:25) as their song filled the jail that evening. And then, all at once, everything changed!

An earthquake so strong that the prison cell doors flung open occurred, and all the prisoners' chains were loosened. I love that this supernatural moment happened right in the middle of Paul and Silas's choice to worship!

Time for a pause

Let's talk about the power of praise.

1. **Praise precedes breakthrough!** Even though it seemed like all hope was lost and everything was stacked against them, Paul and Silas chose to boldly worship God in their lowest moment. Notice that the story is clear about the order of events. It doesn't say first their chains broke, and then they worshipped. No, they worshipped *first*, and *then* their chains broke!

There's a huge difference. If you're anything like me, you might be tempted to praise God only after you've received your breakthrough. But what if it were the other way around?

Some of you are walking through incredibly difficult seasons right now. Heartbreak, loneliness, depression or anxiety, relationship turmoil, financial troubles, eating disorders . . . the list goes on. My encouragement to you is that no matter what you're walking through, worship like you know your breakthrough is just around the corner.

Recently, during a challenging season in my own life, I went for a random walk and God started giving me a new perspective on my struggles. I didn't hear an audible voice or a prophetic word, but as I listened to worship music and sang along in my head, I literally felt my mood shift. I realized I could close my eyes and "get through" the next season, or I could worship *while I waited*.

Isn't it true that worship can change your mood, your posture, and your heart? You stop seeing your circumstances through your own eyes and start seeing them through God's eyes. Worship tunes your heart to beat in sync with God's heart!

Whatever kind of season you're walking through right now, my challenge to you is this: Start worshipping at the top of your lungs while you wait. In your car, on walks, or just in quiet moments while you go about your day. Whatever you're waiting on in life, worship your way through it! Just like Paul and Silas sang songs of praise in jail, I believe we can praise our way to breakthrough, freedom, and a move of God. You can keep waiting in bitterness and frustration, or you can worship like crazy while you wait.

REFLECT ON THIS: In what area of your life do you most need breakthrough?

How anxious do you feel about this area of your life, 10 being the highest level on this scale?

It's time to start praising God! Turn on worship music or sing out loud and just worship for a few minutes. Then write about how your mood, feelings, posture, and/or perspective shifted while you worshipped.

On *this* scale of 1 to 10, 10 again being the highest level, how anxious are you feeling now after this time of worship? *(It's totally OK if your anxiety didn't dramatically change for you. Just keep worshipping!)*

2. **Other people notice when we praise.** Whoa, whoa, whoa. This gets me hype! Did you notice that when the earthquake happened, it didn't loosen only Paul and Silas's chains? It broke *all* the prisoners' shackles!

Scripture tells us that when those shackles broke, all the prisoners stuck around (16:28). They were drawn to what was happening in that room, and they weren't running for their "freedom." I wonder if perhaps they sensed Paul and Silas experienced a far better freedom in Jesus.

Everyone in that prison got to experience a beautiful moment of worship, *and* they got to witness a powerful miracle. Isn't that how things often work in the kingdom? God uses the trials and breakthroughs in our lives as a witness to His goodness and kindness for others.

That's why I believe your choice to praise is about so much more than your own personal breakthrough—your praise can literally and figuratively shift your family, your community, your nation, and even your world.

Even if you feel like life is the best it's ever been for you, what would it look like to worship for other people's breakthroughs? What would it look like to sing a louder song for the needs of those around you? What would it look like to lift your hands for those who can't lift their heads because of the weight of their sorrows? What would it look like to stop caring about how you're perceived while you worship and start caring about what could shift when you worship?

I believe Jesus wants to give you a new freedom in the way you worship. I think He has a new dance for you to dance and a new song for you to sing. It doesn't have to look the way your neighbor, pastor, or friend worships; it can just be intimately sweet between you and Jesus. Don't underestimate the power of sitting in the presence of Jesus and pouring out your praise before Him. It's powerful, it's important, and it's breaking chains all around you.

I could talk about worship all day, but let's get back to our story!

TAKE NOTE: What happened in Acts 16:27–28?

The jailer woke up, and thinking all the prisoners had escaped and imagining his fate when his bosses found out, he panicked and was about to end his own life. Paul stopped him and assured him that none of the prisoners had left. The jailer, shocked, fell at Paul's feet and inquired, "What must I do to be saved?" (16:30).

Even though it's likely the jailer was naive to the full implications of his question, Paul and Silas explained to him that salvation was found through Jesus. He invited the two men to his home as his personal guests and tended to their wounds, and there he and all his family members were baptized. They shared a late-night feast and joyfully celebrated this new life. Later, they returned to the prison in time for their official release, met with Lydia again, and then left town. Just another wild road trip with Paul!

I hope today's Scripture reading encouraged your heart, compelled you to worship, and gave you hope that your breakthrough is on the horizon. No matter what you're facing in this season, remember to simply worship while you wait!

week five: day 4

Filled with the Spirit

Acts 17–19

Today we'll be reading through three chapters in Acts—17 through 19. So you probably don't want a long-winded introduction from me. Let's jump right into things together!

STOP AND READ: Acts 17

TAKE NOTE: What three main places did Paul visit in Acts 17? *(Hint: Use your Bible's subheadings!)*

I hope you noticed that Paul's typical missionary routine played out similarly in each new destination, as we see in Thessalonica and Berea. He preached to the Jews in the synagogue, *caused a stir*, preached to the gentiles, *caused a stir*, and then got kicked out of town.

It took a lot of boldness, conviction, and courage to keep doing the same crazy thing over and over again knowing the result would probably be the same. But even with strong opposition to his teaching, Jews and gentiles alike were coming to know Jesus and the story of His resurrection.

Pay attention to the way Paul taught and went about his ministry. His *message* constantly landed him in trouble, but his *manner* was truly impossible to accuse. Here's what I mean by that: Paul's message of Jesus's resurrecting and His being both Savior and King offended Jews and gentiles alike. They rioted and called the authorities time and time again. Paul would get in trouble, but most of the time, nobody truly knew exactly what his crimes were. He annoyed people with his zeal for his message, but he never offended anyone in manner.

Isn't it true that we sometimes flatter ourselves into thinking we've been radical in message when perhaps we've only been annoying in manner? I see this frequently on social media, where people use a message they feel God has stirred up in their soul as an excuse to exhibit poor manner.

But Jesus didn't say we could expect to be persecuted for our manner; He said we could expect to be persecuted for our message. There's a huge difference between the two! The message of Jesus isn't an excuse to be a bully, curse people who disagree with you, or participate in cancel culture—dismissing people you think just don't seem to get it. Like Paul, let's be people who aren't afraid to offend others with Jesus's message but are fierce in honoring people with a manner that reflects Jesus's character.

REFLECT ON THIS: Have you confused manner and message? How so?

How might you need to refine your manner on certain topics to ensure you don't cheapen your message?

You'll notice Paul's respectful manner during his conversations in Athens with a group of Epicurean and Stoic philosophers. He engaged with their questions, but he didn't shy away from the truth about the resurrection. But what the heck is an Epicurean or Stoic philosopher? (Don't worry, I had to look them up too!) Let's dig for some context about these two people groups. It makes reading Paul's speech to them all the more interesting and powerful.

Epicurean philosophers believed divine beings, or gods, had nothing to do with humanity—that gods and the earth were totally separate. On the other hand, Stoic philosophers were from the school of thought that said all things, both good and bad, were god and there was a spark of divinity in each person.

This explains why they were excited to hear from and debate with Paul. If you read his message to them again, you'll see how he customized his preaching for *both* groups of people while also exposing *both* false ways of thinking. Paul was such a boss for the kingdom!

STOP AND READ: Acts 18

In Acts 18, Paul made his way to the city of Corinth. Pay attention to the names of the places he visited. Many of them would eventually become the recipients of his New Testament letters, also called epistles. Galatia would receive Galatians, and of course Corinth would receive 1 and 2 Corinthians.

What's so cool about studying the book of Acts is that you gain a broader understanding of the rest of the New Testament. You'll be able to recognize names and understand historical context the next time you revisit these letters. It's really so cool!

While in Corinth, Paul befriended a Jewish married couple named Aquila and Priscilla. They'd been living in Rome, but because of a ruling from the Roman emperor Claudius that had banned all Jews from Rome, they were forced to relocate to Corinth.

Aquila and Priscilla were tentmakers by trade. Interestingly enough, so was Paul! (Who knew he had so many talents?) Paul joined their tentmaking business while he taught in the synagogues each Sabbath. To nobody's surprise, opposition started to rise up in the city shortly after. But this time, God intervened (Acts 18:9–11).

TAKE NOTE: What did the Lord say to Paul in a vision (18:9-10)?

This vision from the Lord implies that Paul felt fearful. Something about what was happening in Corinth made him uneasy. Maybe it was the opposition, maybe it was the moral corruption in the city, or maybe his journeys were starting to take a toll on him both mentally and physically. We can't be sure, but it seems to me like God intervened at the perfect moment. He told Paul to keep preaching boldly, that He would be with Paul, and that Paul would have a community of fellow believers in Corinth to strengthen him.

After this vision, Paul stayed in Corinth for a year and a half. Unlike most of his departures, where he was forced out by angry citizens, he finally moved on peacefully because it was the right time.

Throughout Acts, we've seen this truth repeated: God shows up and speaks right when we need Him to. He doesn't come too early or too late; He comes right in the nick of time (and typically with only the *most* important details). I'm sure you're anxiously waiting to hear from God about something in your life. Trust that His voice will speak at the perfect time and in the perfect way.

REFLECT ON THIS: What are you currently waiting to hear about from God?

How has this Scripture given you hope to trust His timing?

I don't want to miss the discipleship of Apollos by Priscilla and Aquila in Ephesus, so let's look again at Acts 18:24–26.

FILL IN THE BLANKS: Acts 18:26

> [Apollos] began to speak boldly in the synagogue. When ____________________ and ____________________ heard him, they invited him to their home and explained to him the way of God more adequately.

I love that the book of Acts mentions this power duo working together in ministry and discipleship side by side. It inspires and encourages me as a married woman to continue looking for ways my husband, Tyler, and I can respond to God's call on our life together. Some of our best and most meaningful moments have happened in ministry when we've chosen to intentionally serve God together.

Single women, I'm telling you, don't settle for anything less than a man whose heart is on fire for God and desires to serve Him alongside you. It's so worth it!

STOP AND READ: Acts 19

TAKE NOTE: What does Paul ask the disciples he finds in Ephesus, and how do they respond (19:2–3)?

While Apollos taught in Corinth, Paul moved on to the city of Ephesus. Upon his arrival, he came across a group of believers who'd received only John's water baptism. Paul told them of a second, more important baptism in Jesus, and they responded eagerly. Paul laid hands on twelve men, and they were filled with the Holy Spirit, immediately speaking in tongues and prophesying.

This is such an interesting passage and story. These men were called disciples, yet they were still missing something. There was more to the story for them to unlock, encounter, and step into—mainly the power of the Holy Spirit.

Every follower of Jesus must eventually pause and assess the Holy Spirit's presence in their lives. Here's what I mean: If you know Jesus and you've invited Him to be your Savior, then the Holy Spirit has permanently taken up residence in you, "a deposit guaranteeing [your] inheritance" (Ephesians 1:13–14). But many of the stories we've studied in Acts talk about men and women being "filled" with the Holy Spirit, which led to all sorts of signs, wonders, and miracles—not to mention revival!

Let's imagine a cup of coffee. There's a difference between that cup *containing* coffee and being *filled* with coffee. If it's filled to the rim, it's obviously full. That's great. But what if the cup is so filled that it's *overflowing*? That's even better!

You see, when a person is filled to overflowing with the Holy Spirit, there's evidence of it! There will be an overflow in your life that's obvious to you and the people around you.

Now, hear me say this: *Being filled with the Holy Spirit doesn't always equal prophesying and speaking in tongues.* God is not a formulaic God! There's no one right way to see proof of the Holy Spirit. The overflow can show up through transformative conversations, supernatural acts of kindness, nudges and whispers in your head and heart, countercultural acts of service, and/or through the more widely known gifts of the Spirit.

I think you can and should ask yourself, *Am I filled with the Holy Spirit?* Now, this isn't an "in-the-Holy-Spirit-club" or "out-of-the-Holy-Spirit-club" question! Think of it more like a gauge or thermometer for an opportunity to get more "filled up." Who doesn't want more of God? That's why I'm constantly asking myself that question and posturing my heart to receive the Spirit.

REFLECT ON THIS: Would you describe yourself as filled with the Holy Spirit? *(This isn't a chance to show off your supernatural encounter résumé. It's simply an honest moment between you and the Lord.)*

At this point in our journey through Acts, how do you feel encouraged and challenged to get "filled up"?

The middle of Acts 19 introduces us to the sons of Sceva, a group of seven Jewish men who tried to practice exorcisms, apparently copying what they'd seen Paul do. As we can see, this didn't end very well for them. It's a great reminder that apart from Jesus and the Holy Spirit, people lack the spiritual power necessary to perform miracles, signs, and wonders. Paul's supernatural abilities came through his relationship with Jesus.

The end of Acts 19 tells about a riot in Ephesus that revolved around money. Isn't it interesting how money (most often "the love of money"—1 Timothy 6:10; Hebrews 13:5) can stand in opposition to the message of Jesus? Paul's teaching about Jesus must have negatively impacted a local silversmith's income from his idol-making business, so he caused a ruckus in the city and stirred up an angry mob. Eventually the city clerk shut the riot down by saying no true offense had been committed. If the locals wanted to challenge Paul, they could take their complaints to a formal court. This effectively dispersed the mob and ended any threat against Paul.

Wow! You made it through quite a lot of studying God's Word today. How are you feeling?

REFLECT ON THIS: What was your favorite thing you read or studied today? What stood out to you the most?

Amazing job! I hope you felt the Spirit's presence in every word you read today. I love that this study is inviting us into fully embracing life in the Spirit together!

GROUP GUIDE

week five

DISCUSS AND REFLECT.

- ★ What part of your Scripture reading this week stood out to you the most and why?
- ★ What did this week's Scripture passage reveal to you about God?

LET'S GET REAL.

- ★ Where do you need breakthrough in your life? How have you been going to God about it? Have you been frustrated or hopeful? What might it look like for you to worship while you wait?
- ★ Thinking back on the story about Paul and Barnabas splitting up, what relationship are you struggling in right now? How do you feel called to make steps toward healing in that relationship?
- ★ Have you confused manner and message? If so, how might you need to refine your manner on certain topics to ensure you don't cheapen your message?

PUT IT INTO ACTION.

Today's activity is simple—to worship! Maybe you have an all-star musician in the group and she can lead you. But for most of us, maybe we can try turning on one of our favorite worship playlists, spreading out, and connecting with God through worship. As we've read, our praise precedes breakthrough!

ACTS 20–24

Mac

week six: day 1

Learning About the Prophetic

Acts 20–21

We're back for another full week of study in the book of Acts. Paul's going to head into Jerusalem to face trial, but before we get there, we'll read about his final goodbyes. I'll give you a quick synopsis since we'll be moving through it pretty quickly.

So last we heard, Paul set off from Ephesus and traveled around visiting the churches he'd already established back in Acts 16 and 17.

When you get to Acts 20:5, notice that Luke enters the story again, joining Paul in Troas along with several other travel companions. In Troas, a young man named Eutychus fell asleep during Paul's long teaching and fell to his death out of a third-story window. Paul attended to him and believed for resurrection through the power of the Holy Spirit. The man lived to tell the story that night. *Wow!*

After the stay in Troas, Paul set sail for Jerusalem, hoping to return in time for the Passover celebration. He made a quick pit stop to speak with the Ephesian elders, saying his final farewells and encouraging them to hold fast to the message of Jesus.

Don't skip over his speech to them! I love verse 36, which depicts their final moment together. Paul knelt to pray with the elders of the church and said a tearful goodbye. The elders wept in grief knowing they quite possibly would never see Paul again. This is real-life stuff!

STOP AND READ: Acts 20

So Paul and the church elders in Ephesus were feeling *all* the feels as they said their final goodbyes. That moment marked a change in the direction of the story of Acts, as Paul sensed he would soon enter into an especially trying season. This was a huge turning point in his ministry.

STOP AND READ: Acts 21:1-6

As chapter 21 kicks off, we see Paul en route to Jerusalem. He and his companions sail through several cities on the way before stopping in Tyre. Paul has his sights set on Jerusalem, but he encountered a little snag as local disciples expressed their thoughts.

FILL IN THE BLANKS: Acts 21:4

> We sought out the disciples there and stayed with them seven days. Through the ____________ they urged Paul not to go on to ____________.

The Spirit told Paul not to go to Jerusalem, but he went anyway. Isn't that a little odd?

Let's unpack this. When you've read this far into Acts (and many of Paul's New Testament letters), it's clear that God had long ago told Paul His intentions for his life and what he would have to endure to fulfill his purpose. God had already told him he was supposed to go to Jerusalem. So why did these men, "through the Spirit," urge Paul not to go?

Some scholars remark that the disciples had good intentions in their warning—suffering was indeed coming for Paul—but their interpretation was incorrect. The disciples in Tyre were likely good, loving, and honoring men and women who loved Paul. Of course they didn't want their friend to suffer! They discerned this prophetic vision of future suffering, and more than likely inferred that it was meant to be a warning for Paul to avoid Jerusalem.

Obviously, I don't know your personal experience with prophetic words or visions. Some of you are probably fairly comfortable with them while others might be wondering what the heck I'm talking about. Let me explain.

Over the course of my life, people have shared with me prophetic dreams, pictures, and words the Holy Spirit gave them specifically for me. I've also received a vision or word from the Spirit that I've felt compelled to share with other people. In my experiences both giving and receiving words, sometimes they hit home and other times they seem to fall flat.

I wholeheartedly believe that even though the gift of prophecy can feel awkward, it's mostly just normal people talking to their Father, asking good questions, and discerning His voice. But as we stretch this spiritual muscle, we won't always get it right. And that's why I think we have to pay attention to this scriptural moment. It's a reminder that we need to use acute discernment when interpreting prophetic words we give or receive.

As you can see, Paul wasn't skeptical of the disciples' prophetic word, and he didn't lash back at them or shut them down. Rather, he simply stayed curious and listened, and we can assume this gave him an extra dose of caution as he continued on his journey to Jerusalem. But what the givers of the prophetic word ultimately interpreted as a message for him to not go, Paul interpreted as another reason he *had* to go.

Whenever you receive or give any message on behalf of the Spirit, I encourage you to engage curiously, intentionally, and humbly as you work it out with Jesus.

REFLECT ON THIS: Have you practiced hearing from God for others? If so, how are you continuing to grow in this? If not, how would you like to grow in this?

What's your biggest takeaway from Paul's response to the disciples' request that he not go to Jerusalem?

STOP AND READ: Acts 21:7–9

Verse 8 tells us Paul arrived in Caesarea and stayed with Philip, whom we already met in Acts 8. Remember, Caesarea is where our friend Cornelius lived (Acts 10).

Time to pause

I want to point out one tiny, easy-to-miss, kind-of-random piece of Scripture here that I love and think you'll love too. Notice what's said about Philip's daughters: "He had four unmarried daughters who prophesied" (Acts 21:9).

Even though the story doesn't say whether these women shared a prophetic word with Paul, Luke thought it was important to add Philip's four unmarried daughters who prophesied into the story. To me, this random verse feels like a little love letter from the Lord, addressed to all you single women as a reminder that you matter and you're noticed in the kingdom.

Each of these four unmarried women (aka *single ladies*!) more than likely had a notable gift of prophecy. If you're single right now and feeling discouraged, just sit with this verse for a second. Let God speak truth, purpose, and validity for this season of your life over you. Let Him encourage the gifts in you that can be strengthened and sharpened in the here and now!

We could easily skip over this verse, but I sense that God has some deep work to do in the hearts of so many of you reading this.

REFLECT ON THIS: Married or unmarried, single or in a relationship, what do you sense God might be speaking to you about your gifts and purpose in the kingdom through this verse?

Flip back over to Acts 2:17. This is part of Peter's sermon at Pentecost when he quoted Joel 2:28. Notice how it says that sons and daughters will prophesy! Philip's daughters were part of the living, breathing evidence that the prophecy was true. God is in the details, y'all!

STOP AND READ: Acts 21:10–16

Here we're introduced to a prophet named Agabus, who also believed he'd heard from the Holy Spirit and gave a really strong pitch for Paul to not go to Jerusalem. But Paul was still confident in the mission that awaited him there.

Are you wondering how Paul could be so bold in this decision even after so many warnings? Well, what Luke tells us in verses 13–14 says it all: "Paul answered, 'Why are you weeping and breaking my heart? I am ready not only to be bound, but also to die in Jerusalem for the name of the Lord

Jesus.' When he would not be dissuaded, we gave up and said, 'The Lord's will be done.'"

Paul was ready and willing to face any consequences for the sake of the gospel, even if it meant death. As you continue reading through the last few chapters of Acts, you'll see that his willingness to literally die for the sake of the gospel impacted every decision he made once he stepped foot in Jerusalem.

The moral of the story is this: God's voice should always be the loudest voice that's guiding our life and decisions. If you truly feel like you've heard from God, like Paul did, you've got to stick to it! Your mom, your friends, your family . . . from the most genuine places in their hearts, they simply want to see you safe and happy. That's great! But as we've been reading, that's not always what God promises or even asks of us! Sometimes His voice will lead us to steps of faith that involve risk, discomfort, and even danger. But He promises to be with us every step of the way.

These prophets were right! Things were definitely about to get tough for Paul. But as we see from our reading today, he was more than ready and willing to face it all for the sake of the gospel.

REFLECT ON THIS: If you were placed in Paul's position and everyone was telling you they heard the Spirit say you shouldn't go, would you still go? Why or why not?

How does Paul's decision translate to your life right now?

Can you think of a time when you let someone dissuade you from doing what you knew God wanted you to do? If so, how would you go about that differently?

week six: day 2

The Impact of Honor

Acts 21

We're taking a snail's pace in Acts 21 because there's too much good stuff to just breeze through it. I have a feeling that if you've read Acts 21 in the past, you probably had zero clue what actually happened in this next portion of Scripture. At first glance it's a very odd situation, but it holds a lot of significance.

Let's dig in!

STOP AND READ: Acts 21:17–26

In verse 17, Paul and his crew had finally arrived in Jerusalem, where they were greeted by their friends and the family of God. Not long after, Paul was made aware of some vicious rumors about him spread around town. Basically, many of the Jewish Christians thought Paul had become anti-Jewish, and they falsely believed he advocated for the termination of popular cultural rituals, like circumcision.

Because we've spent the last several weeks following Paul on his missionary journeys, we know he had no interest in totally abandoning Jewish customs. He actually intentionally made efforts to celebrate the diversity of both the gentiles and Jews while simultaneously fighting for their unity in the body of Christ.

STOP AND READ: Flip over to 1 Corinthians 9:19–23.

Read Paul's words here to the church at Corinth, because they demonstrate his heart and mission toward this very issue. He did all things for the sake of the gospel! In verse 21 we see that Paul point-blank said he had not abandoned the law: "To those not having the law I became like one not having the law (though I am not free from God's law but am under Christ's law), so as to win those not having the law."

TAKE NOTE: What does Paul do in Jerusalem to honor Jews (Acts 21:26)?

Despite the false accusations against him, Paul did something very interesting in response. Instead of boldly defending himself, he took on a posture of humility.

Four men in the community had made a Nazirite vow to grow out their hair, offer sacrifices, and abstain from wine and anything that would make them ceremoniously unclean. (Check out Numbers 6:1–21 if you're curious about this.) Some of Paul's friends suggested he should honor the Nazirite vow by publicly joining the four men in the purification ceremony, as well as paying for their expenses, so no one could continue questioning his loyalty or support of Jewish customs.

Paul agreed to the plan even though he knew it wouldn't have a long-term effect on his outcome in Jerusalem. He could have very easily stayed at a friend's house, hiding away as long as possible, but instead he chose to *honor* the complaints from the Jewish Christians. Instead of arguing with them from a comfortable distance because he knew the accusations were false, he humbled himself and showed his goodwill toward them.

I think we can learn a lot from this seemingly small offering Paul made.

We often do only things we can guarantee will work. We don't want to waste our time on plans that won't give us the outcome we want. Our world is driven far more by achievement than by honor. But here we see Paul obediently "wasting" his time to honor the group of people about to have him beaten and imprisoned. And Paul knew they might do this! He wasn't naive to the fact that this choice put him more at risk and could be the final nail in his coffin.

I wonder if Paul saw this choice as a waste of time. Did he regret his decision to honor them? My guess is no—because Paul knew honor was a powerful currency regardless of how it was received. In fact, honor is most beautiful in the context of strong disagreement. Let's look at his own words from Romans 12.

FILL IN THE BLANKS: Romans 12:10

Be devoted to one another in ______________________.

______________________ one another above yourselves.

Paul knew the kingdom power of honor. He knew honor meant recognizing the God-given value of every person, even if they would ultimately cause him harm.

My own experience has shown me that often in the very midst of trying to bless or honor someone, we'll be ostracized or misunderstood. We have to decide right then if honor is a waste. Is it a waste if it doesn't get us the results we desperately want? Or is unadulterated honor one of the most powerful ways to display God's love for the world?

Let's be honest here. It's easy to honor someone you like, but it's a whole other thing to honor someone who wants to prove you wrong or do you harm. But I believe honor is the sharpest sword we have to cut through the noise of hatred, bitterness, and hostility. Choosing to honor another instead of defending yourself doesn't mean you're compromising your beliefs or that the gospel isn't clear. It means *because* the gospel is so clear, and *because* we stand so firm in our beliefs, we can smack hatred in the face with genuine love. That's honor!

This story about Paul gives us a picture of what it looks like to choose kingdom honor even when it makes zero sense to the world around us, and even when it's the very thing that may bring us suffering.

REFLECT ON THIS: Think about a situation where you chose achievement over honor or being right over being loving. Share about it here.

How could the outcome of that situation or the quality of that relationship have shifted if you'd chosen to honor first?

I've been so encouraged to start shaping a culture of honor in places where I have personal influence—in my family, in my friend group, and at my workplace. I started by first defining biblical honor with two simple, stripped-down values: love and respect.

True love never stops to question worthiness. It's just a knee-jerk reaction when a heart is fully connected and committed to another person. Likewise, true respect never stops to question worthiness but seeks to listen and understand before trying to be understood. Honor looks like leading with love and respect!

It doesn't necessarily mean agreement; you can absolutely honor someone without agreeing with them! And honor doesn't mean watering down truth but affirming the inherent value in the other person before engaging with them.

If you're feeling encouraged or challenged to start creating an honor culture in your own life, here are three reminders I think we can all take away from Acts 21:

1. **Honor without an outcome in mind.** Don't honor people so they'll like you more, do what you want them to do, or change their mind about something. Honor people as a way of pulling out what God has already put in them! What I love about honor is that it often begets more honor. As you honor people with love and respect, they often begin to honor themselves, and then they pay that honor forward to others. When we honor without an outcome in mind, we leave room for the Holy Spirit to surprise us!

2. **Honor first, defend later.** Notice that after Paul heard the rumors about him, he didn't immediately take to the city streets or put an ad in the paper to defend himself. He took on a posture of humility first! When we get to Acts 22, we'll see that he finally got the chance to defend himself and speak the truth. But notice how even his defense was honoring.

When you honor first and defend later, it doesn't mean you're compromising truth. What you're actually doing is paving a way for truth to be better received and noticed. When you defend first, your message is more likely to be disregarded and tossed aside. But when you honor first, you give the other person a chance to take down their walls so your message can be received in its totality. Honor defuses hatred, bitterness, and hostility.

3. **Use honor as a tool to display God's love for the world.** Let's be real. If you're consistently defensive, argumentative, and critical with others, you'll sound like pretty much everybody else in our world. But if you're honoring, loving, and respectful, you'll stand out like a city on a hill!

Honor culture stands in stark contrast to the culture of our world today, which seeks to dehumanize others at every chance. Honor gives us a tangible way to put God's love on display by affirming that every single person has value no matter how we may disagree with them. Let's be so honoring that people are compelled to stop and ask us why. Our immediate response should be that because we're so loved by the Lord, we can be extravagant in how we love others.

REFLECT ON THIS: What's one tangible way you can begin to create an honor culture in the places where you have influence?

After Paul had almost completed the seventh day of the Nazirite vow, he was seized and dragged out of the temple by an angry mob, and "immediately the gates were shut" (Acts 21:30), likely to prevent any potential damage. There's a distinct hypocrisy on the part of the Jews here—they came after Paul in their own sacred place, where worshippers should have been most protected from violence. Clearly, they didn't want to spill Paul's blood in the temple, but it seems they had no problem doing it elsewhere.

Sometimes we shut the gates of the temple in our own lives. Things we would never do inside the walls of the church we do outside those walls, convincing ourselves that God isn't present in it all. But living a life that justifies sin will end up numbing your senses to the presence of God. And even though God will never stop showing up for you, you'll have a lot more difficulty discerning His voice and truth in the midst of the noise and mess you've created in your life.

I think it's important that we take time to examine our hearts and let God search us for any religious hypocrisy that's slipped in without our even noticing.

REFLECT ON THIS: Have you ever behaved differently inside church versus outside of church? Around certain people? Behind closed doors? How so?

How do you think these choices are numbing your senses to God's voice and truth?

Throughout the rest of Acts 21, all hell broke loose! As Paul was being brutally beaten, a Roman soldier intervened and took him into custody. As they took Paul away, he asked to address the angry crowd. (You gotta love Paul—every moment is a moment to share the gospel!)

As you finish reading the rest of this chapter, let the reality of Paul's situation sink in. I know you've probably always thought Paul was a pretty awesome guy, but man, isn't he even better than you thought?

STOP AND READ: Finish reading Acts 21, verses 27-40.

week six: day 3

God's Plan > Your Plan

Acts 22

Yesterday we left off on quite the cliff-hanger! The Roman soldiers had taken Paul, but he wanted to address the angry crowd before he was thrown into jail. Acts 21:35 says these people were so violent that the soldiers had to carry Paul so he wouldn't be beaten to death. Yikes!

But let's see what he had to say.

STOP AND READ: Acts 22:1–21

Paul brought his defense before the crowd as he beautifully reflected on his past, sharing the powerful encounter he had with Jesus on the road to Damascus. Don't you love hearing this story from Paul's point of view?

In verse 19, Paul tells the crowd about a moment when he low-key tried to reason with God. In a vision one day, God told him to leave Jerusalem because his testimony wouldn't be accepted there.

This was Paul's response: "'Lord,' I replied, 'these people know that I went from one synagogue to another to imprison and beat those who believe in you. And when the blood of your martyr Stephen was shed, I stood there giving my approval and guarding the clothes of those who were killing him'" (Acts 22:19–20).

In this conversation, Paul was basically pleading with God to let him go to the Jews instead of to the gentiles. Paul probably thought something like *These are my people! How cool would the before-and-after testimony be? This is the perfect group for me to minister to and make a difference in their lives. I was the most intensely religious, devout one among them, and look at me now! That has to mean something, right?*

Obviously, I'm putting words in Paul's mouth, but it makes me laugh because this legit sounds like so many of my own conversations with God! If you had the chance to read my journal entries when I had a crush on a guy, you'd find they often said something like *Come on, God! I would be so good for him!* (LOL. Embarrassing.)

So Paul told the crowd about his argument with God and that he'd wanted to launch his ministry in Jerusalem by preaching to the Jewish people.

FILL IN THE BLANKS: This is God's response to Paul in verse 21.

"__________; I will send you far away to the ____________________."

God said *go*! He'd already set Paul aside for the gentiles, and although it didn't make sense to Paul at the time, he still responded with obedience.

Isn't it true that sometimes we think we've figured life out based on our biggest strengths or epic plans, and God will be like, *That's really lovely. Now, go . . . somewhere else.* I hate how much I relate to this! I'll get two or three steps ahead of God's plan and tell Him we're taking a left-hand turn, and He's like, *Love your enthusiasm, but we're turning right!*

You told God you'd found "the one," but then you never saw that guy again.

You told God the job was going really well, but He said He had something better.

You told God you wanted to ramp up your schedule and do more crazy things for the kingdom, but He told you to rest.

Isn't that life with God? Frustratingly, beautifully unexpected in the best way possible. We can take some great suggestions for our lives to Jesus—and even try to convince Him—but we shouldn't be surprised when He politely declines the plan and sticks with His much better one.

REFLECT ON THIS: How often do you experience this about life with God?

Never — Rarely — Sometimes — Often — Called Out!

What plan, if any, are you suggesting to God would be best for your life right now—maybe even trying to convince Him? What would it look like to instead surrender to His ways?

STOP AND READ: Acts 22:22–30

For a moment it seemed as if the tension had been defused. The crowd respectfully listened to Paul's message—until he got to the point in the story where God told him to go to the gentiles.

The Jews couldn't believe God would want to include the gentiles in His plans. That stood in the face of their entire belief system; according to the Old Testament, they thought, the Israelites were God's *only* chosen people. Things got out of hand again, and Paul was taken into the soldiers' barracks.

They were about to beat him, but then he pulled out the fact that he was born a Roman citizen (22:25–28)! It was a serious violation of Roman rights to even bind a Roman citizen without first granting them a fair trial and due process. The planned beating was immediately abandoned!

Being born a Roman citizen would've been extremely rare for an educated, devout Jew like Paul. Scholars assume his citizenship was passed down by parents or grandparents who had perhaps been rewarded with it because of good done on behalf of Rome. The Roman commander questioned the validity of Paul's claim, but then he was convinced and released Paul so he could undergo a trial before the Sanhedrin.

We'll get into this a little more tomorrow, but don't get your hopes up. It's a long road ahead for our guy Paul!

week six: day 4

When Your Mission Is on Pause

Acts 23–24

We're picking up in Acts 23 today as Paul is about to undergo trial before the Sanhedrin. Remember, Paul just revealed he had Roman citizenship, which meant he had a chance to speak for himself before they could just mob him.

Let's see how Paul decided to use this opportunity.

STOP AND READ: Acts 23:1–11

Among the crowd were both Pharisees and Sadducees, two people groups with very different theology. The Sadducees would have said there was no such thing as resurrection and that Paul was completely crazy. In contrast, the Pharisees believed in things like angels, spirits, and resurrection. So Paul, hoping to gain some favor from at least some of the people there and get the attention off himself, shared about his background as a Pharisee and his obvious belief in resurrection.

This created quite the uproar between the Pharisees and Sadducees, who started intensely arguing with one another. It eventually got so heated that the troops had to get Paul away from the crowd because it seemed as if he might get "torn to pieces" (23:10).

I love what happens next! In the disappointment, fear, and loneliness of prison, Jesus shows up for Paul.

FILL IN THE BLANKS: Acts 23:11

> The following night the Lord stood near Paul and said, "Take
>
> courage! As you have testified about me in ________________,
>
> so you must also testify in _____________."

This tells us Jesus was still very much looking out for Paul and joining him in his journey every step of the way. Verse 11 says Jesus was physically there with him, which, as we know, was not expected and was unusual for the Lord to do. But Jesus not only showed up for him but gave him words of comfort and affirmation.

As you can imagine, Paul needed to hear this. This was the start of a super long journey, and this encounter with the Lord gave him the courage he needed to continue.

STOP AND READ: Acts 23:12–35

Throughout Acts 23 we start to see a pattern developing. The Jewish leaders would accuse Paul of starting a revolt against Rome, but without any concrete proof to warrant punishment. The Romans had no idea what to do with him! They knew he wasn't a criminal, but he kept claiming that a crucified Jewish man was king, an idea that wouldn't sit well with Emperor Caesar. Paul was about to enter into a long holding period where he appeared before all of these Roman officials awaiting his fate as a prisoner of Rome.

At the end of Acts 23, we read that Paul was transported during the safety of night to Caesarea, where he was kept in the custody of the Roman governor Felix for two years.

STOP AND READ: Acts 24

TAKE NOTE: How many years was Paul in prison (24:27)?

In Acts 24, Felix invited Ananias the high priest and other Jewish officials to come and make their case against Paul. But a decision was never reached, and Paul remained Felix's prisoner for two years until a new Roman governor was appointed.

During this time, Paul's life, mission, and purpose seemed to be on hold. In fact, throughout the remainder of Paul's story in Acts, he entered into years and years of delay. Sure, he was treated well and his friends were allowed to come and go as they pleased, but remember, Paul was a man with great vision and purpose for his life. I imagine nothing bothered him more than sitting around and doing nothing, reliant on the mercy of others.

Sometimes the toughest battles we encounter are less about facing giants and more about facing quiet enemies, like years and years of delay. Satan often does his nastiest work while we're waiting on God to move. He has a lot of time to do subtle damage by sowing tiny little lies into our minds and hearts. These lies often go unnoticed until one day we realize we've drifted so far from the thing God was calling us to wait on that we're not even sure how to find our way back.

We don't know much about what happened during those two years of Paul's imprisonment, but we'd be naive to assume it was all fun and games for him. Paul was a champion of truth known for being on the move. Yet there he waited, day in and day out for two years, for God to fulfill the promise He'd already spoken over Paul. You know the enemy was coming at Paul from every direction!

So how did Paul steward his season of delay? Based on what we know about him, I think it's safe to guess that he was in constant conversation with the Lord. I would bet that he praised and worshipped throughout the nights like he did in the jail cell in Philippi (Acts 16). I imagine that every single day he reminded himself of that encounter with the Lord we read about in Acts 23, repeating the words "take courage" over and over again. I'm certain he stood in confidence of what God had promised so that the enemy's lies couldn't take root in his heart.

When you're in a season of delay, you have a responsibility to devour truth from both the Word of God and the Holy Spirit. You need truth that speaks into your circumstances and truth that rewrites the narratives the enemy tries so desperately to set in stone.

We will all face delays, some of which might even be God-ordained! Will we remain faithful while we wait? Will we fill ourselves with truth or fall victim to the enemy's lies? Will we drift or stand firm?

REFLECT ON THIS: Are you in a season of delay? If so, what have you been filling yourself with while you wait?

What lie from the enemy have you been believing that you need to rewrite with truth?

This is a little bit of a spoiler alert for what's to come, but we later see Paul awaiting his trial in Rome, his life still on hold. He was on house arrest, unable to resume his missionary journeys. But during that time (which you'll read about in Acts 28), he wrote at least four letters (Ephesians, Colossians, Philemon, and Philippians) to some of his friends.

Paul would have reasonably thought his letters might encourage a few people, maybe a dozen max. I often wonder if he had any clue at all about the millions—no, *billions*—of people who would be impacted by his delay. Every follower of Jesus who came after him would devour his words and hold on to them as promises and truth in the midst of their struggles. Paul's story just proves that you never know how God is moving when you think you're standing still.

Paul's life is a testament to how God works in the delays and why it's so important that we stand firm when we feel like our life is on pause.

REFLECT ON THIS: How might God be moving in your life while you think you're standing still?

We're heading into our last week of our Acts study together with Kenz—Week Seven—and we'll see how God continued to move through Paul's life in some miraculous ways.

GROUP GUIDE

week six

DISCUSS AND REFLECT.

- ★ What part of your Scripture reading this week stood out to you the most and why?
- ★ What did this week's Scripture passage reveal to you about God?

LET'S GET REAL.

- ★ What, if any, plan are you suggesting to God or even trying to convince Him would be best for your life? What do you think God might be saying to you instead?
- ★ Have you felt like your life has been a little bit (or a lotta bit) on pause? Can you honestly say you've trusted God's timing in this? Or have you been anxious?
- ★ Which of the three points about honor below do you feel most compelled to grow in? Why?
  1. Honor without an outcome in mind.
  2. Honor first, defend later.
  3. Use honor as a tool to display God's love to the world.

PUT IT INTO ACTION.

Let's practice honor!

At this point in the study, we're hoping you know the others in your group a little better and can pretty confidently share something you admire about every person in the room. Maybe it's a way you've seen them let God move through their life, maybe you want to thank them for something, or maybe you want to point out an awesome part of their character others might have overlooked. One by one, simply love and encourage one another through honor.

ACTS 25–28

Kenz

week seven: day 1

The Pillars of Our Faith

Acts 25–26

Can you believe it? We've reached the final week in our dangerously wild journey together through the book of Acts. It's been an adventure to say the least. We've witnessed the Spirit move time and time again, we've learned so much about the origins of the early church, and we've seen the continuous acts of our risen Jesus.

This week we're closing out our study by reading Acts 25–28, the culmination of Paul's story. We'll also spend some time wrapping up a few of the major themes we've studied throughout the duration of Luke's letter to Theophilus.

Let's get back to Acts 25. Paul was in a season of delay for two years until a new Roman governor was appointed.

STOP AND READ: Acts 25

Festus, the new Roman governor of the province of Judea, traveled to Jerusalem to make some ceremonial political rounds with the hope of stirring up goodwill among the local Jewish leaders. Two years had gone by since Paul's unproductive trial under Felix, and the Jewish leaders were more upset and determined than ever to silence him. They requested that Paul be brought back to Jerusalem for trial, but they had a low-key plot to ambush and kill him along the way!

Festus suggested that, instead, some of the Jewish leaders could travel back with him to Caesarea and try the case there. (Maybe Festus knew of their plot or maybe this was the hand of God keeping Paul under His protection—we don't know!)

The day after Festus arrived back in Caesarea, Paul was brought before him. Festus asked if he would be willing to go back to Jerusalem for trial. Paul knew his next step was in Rome because God had already told him (Acts 23:11), so he made an appeal to Caesar.

Appealing to Caesar was a serious deal, but it was also the right of every Roman citizen to have their case heard by Caesar if the lower courts couldn't reach a decision. Appearing before Caesar would be kind of synonymous with having your case heard by the Supreme Court in our context today.

But before Paul was sent to Rome to appear before Caesar, Festus had him present his case to one more leader, King Herod Agrippa II—as well in front of the king's sister Bernice. Agrippa "was known as an expert in Jewish customs and religious matters" because he was the Roman leader appointed to "oversee the affairs of the temple in Jerusalem and the appointment of the high priest."[1]

STOP AND READ: Acts 26 *(I know it's a lot of reading, but you got this!)*

Time for a pause

So again Paul made his defense and told his conversion story, and I want to point out two things you may have noticed from all Paul's defenses shared over the last several chapters.

1. **Christianity is not at odds with Judaism; it's the fulfillment of the hope of Judaism!** Paul recounted his story to point out that he used to be a deeply devout student of Judaism and the law. He knew it better than most and was even a part of the strictest sect called the Pharisees. Paul lived, breathed, and loved Jewish Scripture, culture, and beliefs! That's why he'd spent a good portion of his life persecuting Christians for what he believed to be blasphemy, and that's why his story is so significant. Through his encounter on the road to Damascus, Paul found that Jesus was the fulfillment of the rescue promised to the people of Israel.

Christianity didn't stand in opposition to the Jewish faith; it was the very hope the Jewish people had been waiting for. Jesus was the promised Messiah! Paul hadn't changed gods, or from his vantage point, even changed religions. He had simply listened, followed, and obeyed God right to the feet of Jesus. Jesus had fulfilled everything from the past while simultaneously changing everything in the future.

The Jewish leaders tried to paint Paul as an off-his-rocker radical when in fact his message about Jesus perfectly fulfilled the very Scriptures they obsessed over. Pretty ironic, right?

2. **The gospel is built on two offensive pillars—the resurrection and the inclusion of all people.** All throughout the book of Acts, these two ideas were the very foundation of every message about Jesus, which got Paul and the apostles in trouble the most. Let's look at what Luke tells us Paul said in Acts 26:22–23: "God has helped me to this very day; so I stand here and testify to small and great alike. I am saying nothing beyond what the prophets and Moses said would happen—that the Messiah would suffer and, as the first to rise from the dead, would bring the message of light to his own people and to the Gentiles."

Paul made it very clear that the Scriptures said two things would happen. First, the Messiah would be resurrected. Second, the resurrection would open the door to salvation for both the Jews and the gentiles.

You'll notice that in the verses immediately following this declaration, Festus finally had it with Paul and accused him of losing his mind from all the learning and knowledge he had (26:24). Not the worst insult to receive, I guess!

You see, the gospel Paul taught and the gospel we know today is built on the same two things: the event of the resurrection and the inclusion of all people. Wherever Paul went, whatever audience was before him, he never shied away from these two messages. He never said, "See, there's this really great guy named Jesus, Son of God, who lived a perfect life, died on a cross for a few of your sins . . . and yeah, that's it! So who wants to be baptized?"

LOL, nope! His message sounded more like "Jesus, Son of God, lived a perfect life, died on a cross for *all* your sins, and resurrected from the grave, defeating death once and for all. Come and be baptized!"

You see, I believe one of the key things God is trying to teach us through Acts is *how to preach the gospel*. In order to learn how to do it, we have to pay attention to what's included and also what's most offensive. So much of Paul's experience is still true for us today. People won't be offended if you tell them Jesus simply lived, was a radical guy, and performed a few miracles. But they *will* be offended (and skeptical) when you tell them Jesus resurrected from the dead for *all* people, including the group they hate most. Resurrection sounds unlikely! A God who wants you to love your enemies feels counterintuitive!

But what did Paul and the apostles say over and over again? *Jesus resurrected for everyone!* So that's how we preach the gospel today even if those two things are exactly what might bring the deepest offense.

One of my favorite Bible teachers, Katia Adams, says this: "We have to trust that the gospel is good seed when it's planted. We have to trust that God knows what He is doing with His own sword. He does not need us to be His own personal PR guru. You don't need to help make Him look a bit better! He tells us what to do and we go do it!"[2]

Yes and amen! We don't have to be God's crisis consultants. His Word is powerful, persuasive, and so good on its own. I hope the book of Acts has given you more confidence to get out there and share the good news of Jesus with the world around you. You don't have to add sparkle, and you don't have to diminish the confusing parts. Just lay it all out there before the people God puts in your path and let Him do the rest!

REFLECT ON THIS: How has Acts encouraged and empowered you to step more boldly into evangelism?

What still makes you nervous?

week seven: day 2

The Storms of Life

Acts 27

If you remember from yesterday, things got a little dicey at the end of Paul's defense presentation before Festus, King Agrippa, and Bernice, but they still found no fault in what he'd done.

In today's reading in Acts 27, Paul, along with several other prisoners, was handed over to a Roman centurion named Julius who was responsible for getting them to Rome.

You heard it . . . they're headed to Rome, baby!

STOP AND READ: Acts 27

REFLECT ON THIS: What about Paul stands out to you from this story?

You might have some random knowledge about Rome from your middle school world history classes, but let me refresh your memory: Rome was the largest and most influential city in the Roman Empire. It was also the major destination implied for Paul since Acts 19.

In verse 3 you'll see that Julius treated Paul well by letting him make a few visits when they landed in Sidon. Did you also notice that Paul was allowed to bring some friends with him on the journey? This included our beloved writer Luke and Aristarchus, a Macedonian from Thessalonica. Julius more than likely gave Paul special favors because Paul wasn't yet a convicted criminal, and more importantly, he was full of the Holy Spirit. His natural kindness overflowed from him as it always did.

Once they'd made it to Fair Havens near the town of Lasea, Paul warned Julius and the crew that their voyage ahead would be "disastrous and bring great loss," including their own lives, because of the weather. He seemed to be implying they should wait in the harbor (27:10). But the pilot and owner of the ship advised Julius to go. Apparently the harbor was "unsuitable" for spending the winter (27:12).

Did you know Paul was an experienced seaman? Prior to this journey to Rome, he'd already traveled around 3,500 miles on the Mediterranean Sea throughout his missionary journeys. If we read his second letter to the church at Corinth, written before this voyage, we'd see he'd already been in three shipwrecks! Paul's suggestion not to sail could have been inspired by the Holy Spirit, or it could have come from his knowledge and experience with sailing the Mediterranean. Or both!

Needless to say, as Paul had predicted, their trip didn't go so well! A violent storm appeared, and for many days and nights their vessel barely survived on the tossing sea. This was when Paul's position on the ship changed. Although he was a prisoner, he took on a new influential leadership role (of course) and shared a message of hope with all the passengers. In a dream God had told Paul their lives would be spared, but first their ship would wreck on an island.

FILL IN THE BLANKS: Acts 27:33

Just before dawn Paul urged them all to eat. "For the last fourteen days," he said, "you have been in ________________ ________________ and have gone without food—you haven't eaten anything."

REFLECT ON THIS: Do the words *constant suspense* resonate with you in a funny way? Why or why not?

TAKE NOTE: What does Paul encourage the men to do in Acts 27:33–34?

I love the moment when Paul broke bread in front of the entire crew and urged them all to sit down and eat. It provided a moment of peace in the midst of a storm, reminiscent of Jesus with the disciples in the upper room at the Last Supper.

Isn't it true that metaphorical storms are pretty much a guarantee when it comes to life with Jesus? Sometimes people seem to be under the false impression that once they have faith, everything will be just peachy. But the entire book of Acts is an obvious reminder that when we walk with Jesus, we can and should expect to face trials, struggles, temptations, and storms of many kinds. The beautiful part of storms is that they often reveal the true depth of our faith and reposition us for what God has for us next.

In the midst of this storm in Acts 27, we see the stark difference between following fear and following faith. Pretty much all the crew members made their decisions based on fear. Paul, on the other hand, listened to the voice of God. Although he couldn't avoid the storm, he received assurance of the outcome.

The storms of our life will always reveal what's really in our hearts. Are you driven by faith or fear? Faith doesn't necessarily mean the absence of fear, but rather knowing you're ultimately safe in the hands of Jesus. In the midst of our storms, we have to trust that God will provide protection, strength, encouragement, and redirection.

REFLECT ON THIS: What storm are you currently facing in life?

What have you seen more of in your heart—faith or fear? Why do you think that is?

Storms don't just reveal our true faith, they also reposition us for God's purposes. When a ship is in a storm, it's inevitable that the ship will move. It cannot physically remain stationary! The same is true in our lives. Storms bring us to a new place God will often use for His good.

We see this in action through Paul's experience. The storm repositioned him as a leader and voice of authority on the ship. This gave him the opportunity to put the gospel and God's goodness on display for every person present. They saw tangible evidence that God was real and that He could protect them from harm. That's powerful! God used the storm to reposition Paul metaphorically speaking, but also physically. Verse 44 indicates Paul's encouragement and God's protection meant all 276 people on board reached the shores of the island of Malta safely.

In Malta, Paul would be given opportunities to continue teaching the gospel. Ultimately, God used the shipwreck that should have been a total disaster to instead show His love to more and more people. No matter what storm you're facing, pay attention to how God might be using it to reposition you physically and spiritually for His calling and purposes.

REFLECT ON THIS: How might God be repositioning you for His purposes in the midst of a storm you're currently facing?

week seven: day 3

An Opportunity to Serve

Acts 28

I know. We are *soooo* close to the very end of the book of Acts, and you might be thinking, *Can we just wrap this up already?* LOL, I promise we'll get there. But before we do, we just can't miss this seemingly random thing that happens once Paul and his fellow prisoners make it safely to the shores of Malta.

It's probably just me, but when I hear the word *Malta*, all I think about is Joey's season of *The Bachelor* when he and fifteen women traveled there in hopes of finding love. I'm wondering if the girls were having conversations about Acts 28 on their way. Do we think they knew what happened on the shores of this island thousands of years ago? Someone send them this study ASAP! (He-he)

Well, very different from *The Bachelor* crew all glammed up arriving on the shores of Malta, Paul and the other 275 people on board were at their wits' end! They were obviously exhausted from the fifteen days at sea, and we can imagine they were fed up with one another and the entire situation. I'm picturing a huge crowd of starving, skinny, raggedy men limping up onto the shores as they're greeted by the islanders.

STOP AND READ: Acts 28:1–10

Luke shares that when the men arrived, it was raining and cold, but the islanders were super kind. They built a fire and welcomed them. Paul, without hesitating, joined in to help!

Mind you, Paul was most likely just as exhausted, if not more so, as everyone else. Plenty of others more suitable to build fires were there—outdoorsy men and soldiers—but Paul stepped up to the plate. As Scripture reads, it seems that almost immediately he joined in to help. Serving God in this way was just second nature to him.

I don't know about you, but I probably would have done at least four different things. One, I would've taken a nap. Two, I'd find some food. Three, I'd spend the next twenty-four hours venting about the stupid sailors. Four, I'd definitely ignore everyone and figure out how the heck to get to Rome. But not Paul! He trusted the journey and found an opportunity to share the good news.

But as Paul gathered wood, a deadly viper came out of nowhere and bit him. (Why do I feel like I'm reading a thriller novel? Who knew Scripture was this exciting?) But Paul didn't let this snake bother him. He didn't scream, "Why, God? I just cannot take it anymore!" He didn't start lashing out at the sailors like, "You guys, help! Get off your butts and do something!" Instead, his reaction was calm and unfazed as he simply shook off the snake and continued helping.

As you read in verse 4, the onlookers were a little shaken up by this. They assumed he must have been a murderer and this snake was the final straw serving justice for what he'd done. But they were quickly proven wrong as he miraculously survived a snake bite that definitely should have killed him. Verse 6 tells us they completely changed their minds and instead thought he was a god.

In the following days the leading citizen of the island, named Publius, invited a few of the shipwrecked crew, including Paul, to come stay and rest at his home. His father had been suffering from a fever and was lying sick in bed.

TAKE NOTE: What did Paul do while he was on the island (28:8)?

Paul took the opportunity to lay hands on Publius's father and pray for healing. Guess what! He was fully healed!

Once again, if it were me, I would've been indulging in every little bit of that estate—the food, the bed, the rest, and a moment of silence away from the crowd. I would've absolutely excused myself from doing ministry as I'd "already put in my hours."

Isn't this true, though? How many of us have said those exact words when presented with a perfect opportunity to share our faith, pray over someone, or simply be the hands and feet of Jesus?

We've said things like

- "I'm on my family vacation, and I don't think it's the best time to share my faith with my brother."
- "I'm leading this week. Can someone else get there early and set up the chairs?"
- "I really just need to prioritize my mental health, so I don't think I need to volunteer at church right now."
- "I'm so hungry. Can we make this prayer quick?"

REFLECT ON THIS: Can you think of a recent moment when you selfishly missed an opportunity to serve the Lord? Name it.

What excuses did you make?

How are you convicted by Paul's approach to ministry now?

You see, Paul didn't need a stage, he didn't need a crowd, and he didn't need the religious leaders to be watching for him to take initiative and serve the people around him. Not only that, but he didn't need to be well rested, he didn't need to be fed, and he didn't need to have any of his normal comforts to serve the Lord.

After this happened, more and more people came to Paul, and the rest of the time he spent on the island essentially became a healing mission, turning a really awful situation into something extraordinarily fruitful. What most people would have seen as a complete waste of time, he saw as just the right time.

This was a random and mostly unnoticed blip of time in the entirety of Paul's story, but I think it might feel a lot like the season of life so many of us are in. Maybe you're in a season that feels like a shipwreck. I wonder if things might turn around if you took the focus off yourself and put it on others. Maybe you're in a season that feels like a detour. I bet you'll see more purpose if you stay present instead of wishing for it to be over. Maybe you're in a season of pure survival mode. I can imagine your days would be better if you began trusting the Lord instead of being so fixated on the whys.

REFLECT ON THIS: What have you considered a setback rather than an opportunity to serve?

How can you be the hands and feet of Jesus in your current season?

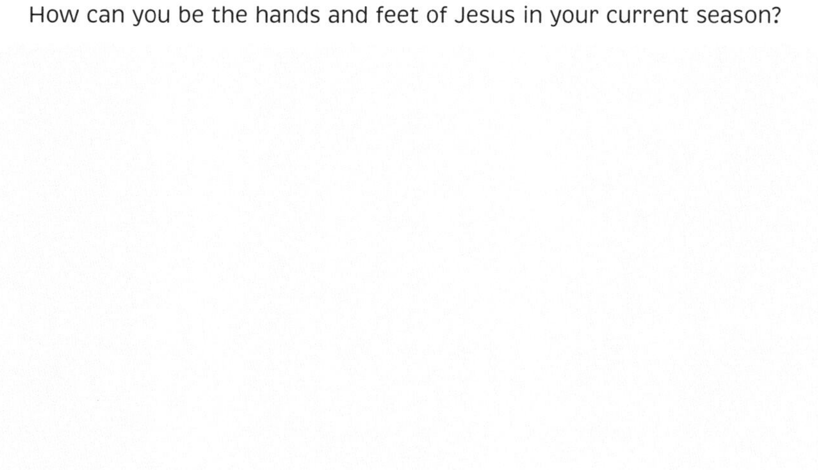

Tomorrow we're closing out our study together . . . *sad!* But the good news is that our guy Paul is back en route to Rome. Let's see what happens there—and what is our role in the mission of Christ today.

week seven: day 4

We Are the Continuation of Acts

Acts 28

We've made it to the final chapter in the book of Acts—*you did it!* I'm honestly so proud of you. That was a whole lot of reading and a whole lot to wrap your mind around, but my hope and prayer is that it's all been worth it. I hope you walk away from this study with more confidence in how God wants to use your life as He used Paul's and the entire early church.

Now, let's get back to the text and finish this thing up.

STOP AND READ: Acts 28:11–31

In Acts 28, the visit to Malta came to a close after three long months of winter. And Paul finally arrived in Rome, where other followers of Jesus greeted him. This signaled to Paul that the faith had spread in Rome, and that his letter to the Roman church had been well received. Quickly, Paul set out to recount the story of his imprisonment and the good news of Jesus to the local Jewish leaders.

You've probably noticed that this missionary journey looked very different from what Paul was used to. As he awaited his trial before Caesar, he lived by himself, guarded by a Roman soldier (aka on house arrest). What's so cool is that it's believed this is when he wrote what are called his Prison Epistles: Ephesians, Philippians, Colossians, and Philemon. It's so classic Paul to take a perceived setback and instead use it as a time to continue advancing the kingdom of God.

Although Paul's *method* for ministry had to change, his *mission* and *message* stayed exactly the same. While he used to go to the local synagogue to speak to the Jews first whenever he entered a new city, here in Rome he had to invite people to come to him due to his circumstances. This was definitely a different tactic than what he was used to, but it didn't deter him from boldly sharing the message God had called him to share.

Remember that in your seasons of delay, your method might have to change, but your mission and message stay the same!

Acts 28 closes like this: "For two whole years Paul stayed there in his own rented house and welcomed all who came to see him. He proclaimed the kingdom of God and taught about the Lord Jesus Christ—with all boldness and without hindrance!" (28:30–31).

And that's it!

Wait. What? Talk about a cliff-hanger! Am I right?

Luke ended this thoroughly detail-oriented story with a, shall we say, less than thorough ending. All we know for sure is that Paul stayed in this house for two whole years, teaching boldly about Jesus to all who would come and listen.

But what happened after that? Did he appear before Caesar? Was he convicted? Was he executed? And what happened to the other apostles in this story? These questions are probably swimming through your brain right now. *Luke, my guy, why would you do this to us?*

While we don't have any concrete answers, I think we have to remember one important thing: The book of Acts was never *really* about Paul anyway. It was about the continuation of all that Jesus did and taught in the lives of ordinary men and women through the power of the Holy Spirit in them. So, yes, Acts is over—but also, Acts continues:

You and I are the continuation of Acts!

Where Paul's story ended, ours is just beginning. We are chapters 29, 30, 31, and so on. (Your life is probably actually something like chapter 5,987,641,921, but that's beside the point!) Our lives are marked by the continuation of all that Jesus did and taught through the power of His Spirit in us.

Remember when at the beginning of Acts we said we have an invitation into the story? The end of Acts 28 is it! We've been invited to join the cast of this story and carry on the next chapters. Our trials, our victories, our miracles, and our journeys are all woven into the story of Acts, a story that pointed to Jesus time and time again!

You are no longer just a bystander or simply a consumer of a good book. You are a vital part of what happens next! So will you accept Jesus's invitation to the adventure and allow Him to continue His life, His message, and His mission through you?

You are John, the beloved disciple of Jesus.

You are Peter, the guy who went from always putting his foot in his mouth to being one of the boldest teachers the church has ever known.

You are Rhoda, the servant girl who accidentally left Peter at the door out of her excitement for how God had moved.

You are Barnabas, the great encourager and developer of kingdom gifts in others.

You are Paul, the fearless evangelist who never offended in manner but always stayed persistent in message.

You are Lydia, the businesswoman who easily recognized Jesus for who He was and opened her home with hospitality.

You are Priscilla, the wife, friend, and tentmaker by day and Spirit-led disciple maker by night.

You are Luke, the quiet bystander who never missed a detail of how Jesus was working and moving.

REFLECT ON THIS: If others were reading about how Jesus worked through you, what do you think or hope they'd read?

Do you feel challenged to surrender even more of your life and heart to Jesus? If so, what would that look like?

Many scholars believe Paul did appear before Caesar and was acquitted of all charges and released. According to early church traditions, he went on to do more missionary work until he was imprisoned again and then executed in Rome around AD 66 or 67.

Just like that, we've reached the end of our wildly exciting adventure through the book of Acts! I'm feeling mixed emotions—sad, happy, and expectant for what's next.

My hope is that throughout this journey, you've fallen head over heels in love with God's Word, and that you now see yourself as fully empowered to walk in the beautiful and mysterious power of His Spirit.

My prayer is that, just like Paul during his house arrest in Rome, we will welcome everyone graciously into our lives, proclaim the kingdom, and teach about our Savior Jesus with boldness and without hindrance.

Thank you for letting us guide you on this journey. It's truly been one of the greatest honors of our lives to sit in the metaphorical back of the raft steering us all through the last seven weeks. Please always remember that you are so loved and cherished by Jesus, and that you have a huge community of faith cheering you on every step of the way.

Let's close this out in true Paul fashion:

> May the grace of the Lord Jesus Christ, and the love of God, and the fellowship of the Holy Spirit be with you all. (2 Corinthians 13:14)

GROUP GUIDE

week seven

DISCUSS AND REFLECT.

- What part of your Scripture reading this week stood out to you the most and why?
- What did this week's Scripture passage reveal to you about God?

LET'S GET REAL.

- Has your life honestly felt a little bit stormy recently? Have you felt like you've been in "constant suspense"? How can you reconnect with God in this season?
- Can you identify a moment or opportunity you missed to serve someone around you because you were honestly frustrated to be there to begin with? What was that thing and how would you do it differently?
- After reading the entire book of Acts (wow, crazy!), what in your life do you feel most excited to surrender and see God move through in new and greater ways?

PUT IT INTO ACTION.

Reflection time!

To wrap up this group time, we thought it would be fitting to reflect on all we've learned. But rather than just spilling out a bunch of information, maybe take a moment to individually flip through the pages of your study and find something that *most* stood out to you. Something that convicted you the most, the crazy cool revelation you had, the moment God spoke to you . . . Whatever it is, share that thing with the group and how you want to continue living into it.

About the Authors

MacKenzie "Mac" Bridges and **Mackenzie "Kenz" Durham** are the passionate cofounders behind Delight Ministries, an organization that provides Christ-centered community for college women at two hundred–plus universities across the United States. As cohosts of the *For The Girl* podcast, best friends Mac and Kenz bring warmth, wisdom, and big sister advice to women in their twenties seeking to follow Jesus. They are also the authors of several beloved Bible studies, including *In My Feels* and *The Wild Invitation*.

Mac currently lives in Charlotte, North Carolina, with her husband, Tyler, and their daughter. Kenz lives in Vero Beach, Florida, with her husband, Josh, and their two kids. Outside of ministry, Mac and Kenz hope to be besties until they're old and gray while still peeing their pants from laughing together on the daily.

CONNECT WITH MAC AND KENZ

ForTheGirl.com

@theforthegirl

@forthegirl___ | @macleighbridges | @kenzraedurl

Notes

Week One Day 1

1. R. Kent Hughes, *Acts: The Church Afire*, ESV edition (Crossway, 2014).

2. The Editors of Encyclopaedia Britannica, "Pentecost," *Britannica*, https://www.britannica.com/topic/Pentecost-Christianity.

Week One Day 3

1. David Guzik, "Acts 2—The Holy Spirit Is Poured Out on the Church," *Enduring Word*, September 28, 2020, https://enduringword.com/bible-commentary/acts-2/.

2. Hughes, *Acts: The Church Afire*, 21.

Week Two Day 3

1. "New Shifts in Church Engagement Trends," Gloo and Barna Group study, Religion News Services, March 13, 2025, https://religionnews.com/2025/03/13/new-shifts-in-church-engagement-trends/.

Week Two Day 4

1. N. T. Wright, *Acts for Everyone: Part One—Chapters 1–12* (Westminster Press, 2015), 80.

Week Three Day 2

1. Ervin Budiselić, "The Impartation of the Gifts of the Spirit in Paul's Theology," *Kairos: Evangelical Journal of Theology* 5, no.2 (2011): 245–70, https://hrcak.srce.hr/clanak/109009.

Week Seven Day 1

1. David Guzik, "Acts 25—Paul's Trial Before Festus," *Enduring Word*, February 3, 2020, https://enduringword.com/bible-commentary/acts-25/.

2. Katia Adams, "A Study of Acts," lecture, https://julianadams.teachable.com/p/a-study-of-acts-katia-adams. Accessed November 19, 2020.